Long-Distance
Grandma

Also by Janet Colsher Teitsort
Treasures for Teachers
Rainbows for Teachers
Seasons of Laughter for Teachers

Long-Distance
Grandma

*How to Stay Connected
with Grandkids Far Away*

Janet Colsher Teitsort

 Baker Books

A Division of Baker Book House Co
Grand Rapids, Michigan 49516

Published by Baker Books
a division of Baker Book House Company
P.O. Box 6287, Grand Rapids, MI 49516-6287

Printed in the United States of America

Library of Congress Cataloging-in-Publication Data

Teitsort, Janet Colsher.
    Long-distance grandma : how to stay connected with grandkids far away / Janet Colsher Teitsort.
        p.   cm.
    ISBN 0-8010-1165-5
    1. Grandparenting. 2. Grandparent and child. 3. Separation (Psychology) 4. Creative activities and seat work. 5. Holidays. I. Title.
HQ759.9.T45   1998
306.874'5—dc21   98-5523

For current information about all releases from Baker Book House, visit our web site:

                http://www.bakerbooks.com

To
Jehovah-shammah
(the LORD is there)
and
John,
my life partner
in parenting and grandparenting

Long-Distance Grandma

Why God? Why did they
have to move?

We've always been
a close-knit family,
always together.
Maybe not in the same house,
but in the same town.

I guess I took
it for granted.
I thought it
would always be.
But now the
mobility of
this century,
the flight of the
young, has touched
my cherished nest
and robbed me of
my grandchildren.

I know you are
sovereign and that
nothing happens
to me, or mine,
until it has first
been filtered through
you. I know there
is a purpose in
their move.

But how can I
be a long-distance
grandma? I can't
even conceive of
such an idea.
I want to bake them
cookies and kiss
their skinned knees.
I want to listen
to their heartaches
and share their joys.
I want to attend their
programs and tell
the person next to
me that the angel
in the third row is
my grandchild.

My greatest fear
is that I won't know
them, nor they me.
Please don't let
that happen. Instead,
grant me your
wisdom to handle
this situation.

I guess I can still bake
cookies; I'll just
have to mail them,
and I can send
those novelty
Band-Aids for
their skinned knees.
They'll be sure to
think of me then.

It's time to revive
the by-gone art of
letter writing.
And I'll
call sometimes, just
to talk to them.

And the programs,
they can videotape
or send snapshots.
We'll keep the
postal services
in business. It
will be fun for
them to get packages.

What a God of
inspiration you are!
It will be okay,
just different.
Cause me to
remember daily
that you who are
present will be
caring for us all.

Contents

May

June

July

Preface

bout six years ago my daughter and son-in-law announced that due to job changes they would be moving to another state. It was bad enough that they were moving, but they were taking my precious grandbabies too. The youngest was a tiny newborn. I was deeply distraught. I had always been fortunate to live in the same small town with my extended family. My own grandparents had lived close by.

As I thought about the upcoming move, I realized we are living in a different age. We send our children off to college, hoping they will find fulfilling careers and have financially secure lives. We shouldn't be surprised when they have to move to different locations to find jobs.

I shared my sad news with my hairdresser. She reminded me of an important truth: God is omnipresent. The same God would be watching over both households. The same sun, moon, and stars would be shining on every member of my family. The same sky that shields them would be providing a canopy over me. What a comfort! A passage in Jeremiah zeroes in on this fact. "Am I a God who is only in one place and cannot see what they are doing? Can anyone hide from me? Am I not everywhere in all of heaven and earth?" (Jer. 23:23–24 TLB).

My greatest fears as a long-distance grandma were that the baby wouldn't know me and that the others

15

would forget. But that hasn't happened. We've kept in touch even though my daughter's family now lives several states away.

Let me be the first to say that nothing can take the place of tender hugs and togetherness shared by grandparents and grandchildren. But if you or your children and grandchildren are hopscotching across the country due to job changes or for health reasons, you have to do the next best thing. You have to become a long-distance grandparent.

You've lived long enough to know that change is inevitable. What you do with change will shape your life and the lives of your family members. You can become disgruntled and depressed, or you can be innovative and make change work for you and your loved ones. Using just a little ingenuity, the extended family can be revitalized and strengthened.

In Romans 8:28 we read, "And we know that in all things God works for the good of those who love him, and have been called according to his purpose." Give the miles between you and your grandchildren to the Lord. He can work them for your good. Nothing in the relationship will be taken for granted. Every contact between grandparents and grandchildren will be treasured.

Here are some factors to consider when making your plans:

1. How often will you be able to see your grandchildren: once a month, once a year, every two or three years? This will help you decide how often you will contact them.

2. What are the ages of your grandchildren? Small children need to see a face and hear a voice. Older children do well with writing projects.
3. How many grandchildren do you have? Are they all in the same household or are several families involved? The number of children and families will affect the amount of packaging, mailings, time, and expense involved.
4. How are your finances? Are you still working or are you living on your retirement fund or social security? Your financial situation will affect the type of projects and contacts you can make with your grandchildren.
5. How busy are you? You should also consider the schedules of your grandchildren. Today's children have busy lifestyles too. Be sure not to over-extend yourself or your grandchildren.
6. How is your health? Will you need help with correspondence, shopping, or mailing? If so, you may want to keep the projects simple. Cards and letters touch hearts and add depth to relationships.
7. Take into account your personality and temperament. Are you organized or are you a procrastinator? It is important to know yourself so that you can make realistic plans and experience success.
8. Do you have access to a computer, e-mail, fax machine, camera, photocopier, camcorder, VCR, tape recorder, or other items to help you with your long-distance grandparenting?

After answering the above questions you are ready to make a tentative plan. Set aside a calendar to be used exclusively for your planning.

All of us collect experiences as we go along, and we really don't know where we get some of our ideas. Recipes and craft ideas are passed from one friend to another like folktales. Many have gone before me with similar ideas, and effort has been made to give credit to original sources whenever traceable. My purpose in writing this book has been to provide grandparents with a jam-packed idea book for long-distance grandparenting.

Many have cheered me on during the writing of this book. To the encouragers—those who have prayed and listened as I planned—please accept my deepest gratitude. I extend a special thank-you to Judy Chatham for her valuable input and for her vote of confidence. A huge thank-you goes to my husband, John, for helping me with the proofreading and editing. Your skill is greatly appreciated. May God grant each of you the desires of your heart.

If you are a long-distance grandma, then this is a book for you. Walk with me through the months, choosing activities for long-distance grandparenting. Your relationship with your grandchild is worthy of nurturing. The activities are varied and will add dimension to your relationship. No longer will you need time to get reacquainted after lengthy separations. You will have kept in touch.

The journaling pages are for your convenience: Write down the cute things that only your grandchild says. Record the activities that you do for each grandchild, and write down your unique ideas. Embark on a learning experience that will bless the entire extended family. Learn to be a long-distance grandparent.

January

anuary is a time of new beginnings. The glistening squares on the new calendar gleam with snowy whiteness, unblemished by forthcoming appointments. Life silently invites you to write upon its pages.

Maybe the sun is shining, and you're feeling positive. Maybe it's cloudy, and your spirit is as downcast as the weather. Perhaps you were fortunate enough to spend the holidays with your grandchildren, or perhaps not. Either way, you're probably wondering when you'll get to see them again. If this description fits you, take heart. This book is for you. I invite you to embark on a new adventure—grandparenting by long distance.

Fun with Photos

Begin the year by taking snapshots of the outside of your home. If you live in a wintry climate, take a picture when there's snow. Maybe you can talk Grandpa into helping you make a snowman for the photo. Then go to the camera department of a store and purchase self-adhesive postcards. They are very inexpensive. Using the snapshots, make postcards of your house to send to your grandchildren. Plan to do this at the beginning of each season. Send older grandchildren their own pack of adhesive cards. They can choose from their favorite photographs and make postcards to send to you. If possible, include some stamps.

You can also take pictures of you and Grandpa as you go through your daily routines. Capture scenes from a variety of rooms in your house. This will enable the grandchildren to get a feel for what Grandpa and Grandma's house looks like. You can use these photos to make more postcards.

If you have access to a computer and photocopier, you can be even more innovative. Make a calendar sheet for each month. Be sure to write in birthdays, anniversaries, and other special occasions for the entire family. Using legal-sized paper, arrange three or four snapshots at the top of the page. Add the appropriate month at the bottom of the page and then photocopy. A smaller version can be created using letter-sized paper. Reduce calendar pages to fit on half a page and add only one or two photos per page. There are many ways to bind the sheets. You can machine stitch across the middle or staple. Many schools and offices have machines for spiral binding. Spiral binding is inexpensive, easy, and gives a professional touch. Make a calendar for each grandchild. The children will love it.

If you don't have time to create your own calendar, check out the camera department where you get your film developed. Many photo labs print calendars using photographs.

Chinese New Year

January is also the month to celebrate the Chinese New Year. Grandchildren can gather information from their library or computer. You get an A+ because you will be contributing to the education of your grandchildren as well as providing a fun experience.

Begin this activity by buying a box of fortune cookies and some chopsticks. These items can be purchased at a grocery store or a specialty store. If you don't have any success finding them, try your local Chinese restaurant. The management will probably sell you a few pairs of chopsticks if you explain why you need them.

Along with the cookies and chopsticks, mail the following recipe for mock chow mein:

Mock Chow Mein

1 pound of hamburger, browned	1 can of chop suey vegetables
1 cup of rice, prepared	1 can of sliced water chestnuts
1 can of cream of mushroom soup	1 package of chow mein noodles

Mix all the ingredients together except the noodles and place in a casserole dish. Heat in the microwave or on top of the stove. Top with chow mein noodles.

This is a very mild Chinese dish. You may add soy sauce for flavoring, but I've found that it works best to introduce children to Chinese food by using this American version. The meal is so quick and easy to prepare that older grandchildren can fix it.

Hot Chocolate and Movie Night

The snow is swirling outside and you've been stuck in the house all day. Perhaps you are spending the winter in the sunny South and are thinking about the grandchildren who live in a northern state. Either way, when dusk approaches and the supper dishes are finished, it's time to relax. But first you have to set the stage.

Mail a mug for each grandchild, along with hot chocolate mix. Stir up your own brew by making the following recipe.

Homemade Hot Chocolate Mix

1 pound of Nestle Quik (If you like a lot of chocolate, add another 1/2 pound.)

1 pound of powdered sugar

1 medium container of powdered creamer

1 medium box of dry Carnation Instant Milk (I recommend that you don't substitute the brand of milk.)

Mix the ingredients together in a big pan using a slotted spoon to stir. The above amounts will make between five and six quarts. Use a canning funnel to fill jars or put the mixture in sealable plastic bags to mail. Include directions for mixing: Add three to four heaping tablespoons to a mug of hot water. Delicious! This mix is guaranteed to warm you to your toes.

Are you pressed for time? If so, buy prepared packets of hot chocolate mix. Mail the packets along with a video of your favorite classic. Check out an extra copy of the same movie from your local library so you can sip hot chocolate and watch the movie at the same time your extended family is watching. Before the movie begins, close the drapes and imagine (you may not have to) a wintry night. Snuggle in and let the evening wrap you and your grandchildren in closeness of spirit.

Story Time

Story time—or at least you would like for it to be. Your arms are aching to enfold those little ones on your lap. You long to read them a story. Not possible? Then do the next best thing. Make a tape. Select books that fit the winter season, or just choose your favorites. Record the stories on cassette tape, reading slowly. Be sure to tell the grandchildren when to turn the page. Send the tape along with the book or books. This makes a great gift for bedtime. The grandchildren get to hear Grandpa's or Grandma's voice as they drift off to sleep. You may also choose to make a videotape of you reading a story. Cassette tapes are nice for bedtime, while watching a video is a nice daytime activity.

A great January book is *The Mitten,* adapted and illustrated by Jan Brett (Scholastic). Several versions of this Ukrainian folktale exist. Check your local bookstores and discover your favorite. If your grandchildren live in a cold climate, you may want to send some mittens to ward off the winter's chill.

Another book that warms the heart is Maurice Sendak's *Chicken Soup with Rice* (Harper & Row). This rhyming book tickles the ear and is a delight to read. *Chicken Soup with Rice* is not only fun, it's educational. It teaches the months of the year—perfect for January!

Be clever and expand on this soup idea. You might pack some soup mugs and dry soup packets along with the book. Instant lunch via long-distance Grandma! Or you can send a recipe for chicken soup. The time to start a recipe box for your grandchildren's future home is when they are young. Most children like to assist their mom with meal preparation as soon as they are old enough. Periodically mail copies of a favorite recipe to each of your grandchildren. The following soup has been known to shoo away wintry colds.

Grandma's Chicken Soup

4 boneless chicken breasts	salt and pepper to taste
1 small package of egg noodles	4 carrots
4 potatoes	1 small can of chicken broth
1/2 tsp poultry seasoning	2 stalks of celery
1 medium onion	

Pressure cook or stew the chicken in water. Remove the chicken and dice; add it to the broth. Canned broth may be added if needed. Peel, dice, and boil the potatoes, onions, and carrots. Precook the noodles. Add all the ingredients to the broth and season. Simmer for a few moments, letting ingredients blend together.

If you want the soup to go perfectly with the book, add a cup of precooked rice.

Winter time for most of us means snow time. *Mrs. Toggle's Zipper* by Robin Pulver, illustrated by R. W. Alley (Four Winds Press), is a fun book about a stuck zipper. Most children have encountered this problem and will identify with the story.

Young grandchildren love being read to, but as grandchildren develop writing skills, try this round robin idea. Grandpa or Grandma begins the round robin story by writing a couple paragraphs. They mail the story to the oldest grandchild, who writes a paragraph or two, then passes it on. If several grandchildren in one family are old enough to participate, the letter circulates within the home. These grandchildren mail the letter on to cousins, or if there aren't any, it goes back to the grandparents. At the end of the year, make photocopies of the completed story for family members. Include the copies with your Christmas cards.

Jigsaw Puzzles

Another winter pastime I remember from my youth is fixing jigsaw puzzles. Buy the same puzzle for each family of grandchildren. Mail the puzzle along with some microwave popcorn packets. Set up the card table and pop the corn. Then all of you can work on the same puzzle, sharing your progress via telephone, e-mail, or letters. Who says you have to be in the same house to participate in togetherness?

Prayer Request Letters and Devotionals

You've heard the adage "The family that prays together, stays together." Grandparents would be wise to take this proverb to heart. Start a family prayer request letter by having all members of the family mail their prayer requests to you. Type up a letter of the requests and mail a copy to each family member. Decide how often you will publish this letter and give family members a due date for requests. Remember to record when and how God answers the prayers. Faith will increase as you and your family see God at work.

Reading from the same devotionals provides another way for families to stay close. Most churches provide quarterly devotionals. Order extra copies and send them to your children and grandchildren. Encourage each other as the weeks go by. The devotions will provide you with topics to share in your letters and phone conversations. This is a great way to encourage spiritual growth.

By now you know who keeps the United States Postal Service in business—grandparents! I must insert a

word of caution here, though. Select a few of the grandparenting ideas to do each month. If you try to do them
all, you will experience a stress level that will send you
into outer orbit. Instead, choose the projects that
appeal to you and yours. Start small and pick up speed
with experience. Hopefully, my ideas will spark ideas
of your own, and you'll develop your own list of unique
grandparenting ideas. Use the journaling pages for
your record keeping.

Happy grandparenting!

Happy New Year!

Journaling Pages

Our three-year-old grandson asked, "Grandma, are you a grown-up?"

"Yes, hon, I am."

"Well, I thought I was, but Mom says I'm not. She says I have to drink my milk in the kitchen."

Wait 'til you hear what my grandchild said . . .

Here's a bright idea for long-distance grandparenting . . .

Name of grandchild

Long-distance activity

Date completed

Name of grandchild

Long-distance activity

Date completed

Name of grandchild

Long-distance activity

Date completed

Name of grandchild

Long-distance activity

Date completed

February

ebruary is the bridge that connects frosty January with the coming of March and the arrival of spring. St. Valentine's Day arrives, and again the month serves as a bridge, this time connecting hearts. It is a time of tenderness when we pause to tell our family and friends how much they mean to us.

St. Valentine's Day

Red hots, miniature candy hearts, lace doilies, aluminum foil, and construction paper fill us with nostalgia of long-ago St. Valentine's Days. We remember the excitement of creating valentine boxes in which our classmates placed cards. Today most schools have resorted to decorating paper sacks or using file folders. The elaborate production of the valentine box has become a thing of the past. Grandparents can revive this art by sharing a story about a valentine box they created.

Crafts

Purchase some lace doilies, construction paper, foil, tape, glue, and children's scissors. Then make a videotape showing you creating a beautiful master-piece and reminiscing of days gone by. Mail the video-tape, along with the supplies, early in February. Your grandchildren will be challenged by your creativity and will want to try their hand at making their own boxes.

Older grandchildren may not want to make a valen-tine box, but they will still enjoy hearing about your childhood memories of St. Valentine's Day. Include a craft project on the videotape just for them. One proj-ect that is challenging and definitely for older teens involves melting candles to make scented hearts.

Scented Wax Hearts

2 scented votive candles
   (one for each heart)
clay cookie mold (heart shaped)
electric potpourri pot or a tin can
   placed in a saucepan of water

small amount of narrow ribbon
nail or other sharp object
   to form a hole in the wax

Melt the candles in a potpourri pot. If you are using a tin can, place the candles inside the can and place the can in a saucepan of water. Heat on low until the candles melt. Discard the wicks. Pour the melted wax into the mold. When the mold is almost cool, punch a hole at the top of the heart to thread the ribbon through. Finish cooling the mold to room temperature and then place it in the freezer for a minute or two. Be sure it is thoroughly cold—not frozen. Turn the mold upside down and the newly formed heart will pop right out. Thread enough ribbon through the hole so that it makes a large loop for hanging. Attach a verse such as Ephesians 5:2. "Be full of love for others, following the example of Christ who loved you and gave himself to God as a sacri-fice to take away your sins. And God was pleased, for Christ's love for you was like sweet perfume to him" (TLB).

As you videotape this project, stress safety features. Accidents can happen using hot wax. But as the grandchildren get older, you have to give them projects suitable for their age. Use your judgment regarding the suitability of this craft for a particular grandchild.

Sweatshirts are another creative way to celebrate St. Valentine's Day. Visit your fabric store and explain that you would like to make decorative valentine sweatshirts for your little ones. The sales clerk will fix you up with all the right supplies. With preprinted fabric and adhesive bonding material, even those who are not expert craft makers can produce some clever creations. Ordinary sweatshirts become something special when Grandma adds her crowning touch.

After age five or six, however, your grandsons will appreciate a plain sweatshirt. They may be too polite to say so, but trust me. I teach in a public school. This also holds true with most pre-teen and teen girls. They'll appreciate your thoughtfulness, but cute sweatshirts are not popular after a certain age. Use this idea when your grandchildren are toddlers, or for elementary-age granddaughters.

Treats

Want to melt the hearts of the younger grandchildren and cause them to get all gushy toward Grandpa and Grandma? Mail them a box of those little candy hearts with the cute sayings. These treats are still relatively inexpensive, but they fill the hearts of grandchildren with tenderness.

"Mommy, Daddy, read this to me!" becomes the cry of the day. It's as if Grandpa and Grandma have written the sweet sayings upon their hearts.

You also can't let February go by without making some valentine cookies. There are many ways to follow through with these sweet treats. Remember to consider your schedule and personality, then proceed.

I love crafts, but I've never had much luck with cookie cutters. Stirring up that batch of sugar cookies is a cinch, placing the cutter on the dough goes smoothly, but the next step is a nightmare. The dough clings. It doesn't know the meaning of the word release. I know what you are thinking—she doesn't use enough flour. I'm telling you that when I use enough flour for the dough to give way, the cookies end up tasting like paste.

Through the years I've tried and tried. I don't give up easily, but I know when I'm defeated. Long ago I decided to forego the time-honored sugar cookie tradition. Sometimes I cheat and buy the rolled cookie dough in the dairy case, but I even have trouble with that. I usually end up slicing the dough and adding sprinkles.

If this type of cookie is your thing, by all means videotape this baking endeavor. Maybe you'll be able to save your grandchildren from my mistakes. In fact, maybe you'd better send me a copy of your videotape. I might be tempted to try just one more time.

My favorite "can't fail" recipe is for Snickerdoodles. They turn out perfect every time, unless you burn them. The recipe can be doubled and it makes dozens. Roll them in cinnamon and sugar or colored sugar. They turn out yummy and your grandchildren will never have to know you are a sugar cookie failure. Here's the recipe that makes me look good.

Snickerdoodles

2 sticks of margarine	3/4 tsp soda
1 1/2 cups of sugar	pinch of salt
2 eggs	2 3/4 cups of flour
2 tsp cream of tartar	

Mix 1 tbsp cinnamon and 1 cup of sugar in a separate bowl

Blend the margarine, sugar, and eggs. Add the cream of tartar, soda, salt, and flour to the blended mixture. When the dough is thoroughly mixed, form it into balls the size of small walnuts. Roll the dough balls in the mixture of cinnamon and sugar or colored sugar. Bake eight to ten minutes on an ungreased cookie sheet at 400 degrees. Don't be alarmed to see the centers of the Snickerdoodles rise then fall during baking. This is what they are supposed to do. This recipe yields four to five dozen cookies.

If you are short on time, try this quick and easy way to send valentine treats. Send a box of graham crackers, canned frosting, candy sprinkles, plastic knives, and valentine napkins. The little ones will love decorating their own valentine delights. When this box arrives, it's so warm and loving that it feels as though Grandma came with it.

Bible Verse Collection

Since February is the month for valentines, which express our heartfelt feelings, it is also the ideal time to begin a collection of Bible verses that have touched the individual hearts of family members. Collect the verses by your chosen method of communication. Perhaps you can persuade family members to share why a particular verse is special to them. Then assemble the verses in a way that can be shared.

Booklets are nice and can easily be printed on the computer, or you may choose to put the pages in a photo album. Needlepoint and calligraphy are possible methods to use when displaying verses. You might want to consider printing a collection of verses, then matting and framing them.

Personally, I want to embroider a Bible verse quilt. I plan to enter the family name and date on the center square. Individual squares will have the name and age of each contributor. Cross-stitch or marking pens could also be used on quilt squares. Someday I will be retired, and I will begin my stitching. If I have to pass my quilt on to the next generation to finish, that's all right. Today I will begin gathering my verses.

Books and Games

February is filled with special days, beginning with Groundhog Day. The month may be our shortest, but it is not short on celebrations. Both Abraham Lincoln's and George Washington's birthdays fall within this month. Many books on the market relate stories about these two men. Make a cassette tape with Grandpa and Grandma reading a story or two apiece. Mail the tape along with the books. Be sure to include some books for the older grandchildren to read.

The month speeds by rather quickly unless the weather has everyone housebound. Grandpa can step in and liven up the gray days of winter. Set up a chessboard in a spot where it can stay. Decide on the players and the game may begin. Players can phone, fax, or e-mail their moves. Letter writing could make the game last all year—a little too long. This game playing method is ideal for the pre-teen or teen grandson. Sometimes grandsons are bored with Grandma's craft and cooking ideas, especially if they're not interested in those types of projects. Not into chess? Number the squares on a checkerboard and proceed in the same manner. Battleship is another game that works well when you use the assistance of modern technology to communicate moves.

If you don't have access to computers or fax machines and frequent phone calls are out of the question, buy the same crossword puzzle book for you and your grandchild. Share your progress by letter. The important things are keeping in touch and sharing an interest.

Bridge the miles as you touch hearts!

Journaling Pages

Our young grandson climbed up on my lap. I gave him
a big smooch and said, "I love you bunches!"
Hugging me, he countered, "Enough to take me outside?"

Wait 'til you hear what my grandchild said . . .

Here's a bright idea for long-distance grandparenting . . .

Name of grandchild

Long-distance activity

Date completed

Name of grandchild

Long-distance activity

Date completed

Name of grandchild

Long-distance activity

Date completed

Name of grandchild

Long-distance activity

Date completed

March

*B*lustery or gentle March winds blow, lifting our spirits upward like Mary Poppins. The gray shades of winter miraculously give way to the variegated greens of spring, and with spring comes hope. Hope is a strong word that rings with promise. Hope for a meaningful relationship with our grandchildren is what motivates us to make the effort to bridge the miles.

The Luck of the Irish

The Irish knew about hope. Hope for a better life caused many of them to immigrate to America. Because St. Patrick's Day falls during March, this month is the ideal time to share information about Irish ancestry with the younger generation.

Visit the library or use your home computer to view a map of Ireland. If your ancestors are from Ireland, mark where they lived and note when they arrived in America. This is the perfect time to do a study of Ellis Island and what it was like for all immigrants arriving in America. The depth of your study will depend on the age of your grandchildren.

Sharing Irish blessings is a fun thing to do with older grandchildren. There are many of them floating around.

Some may have been used over and over within your family. One such blessing is:

> May the road rise to meet you.
> May the sun shine warm upon your face.
> May the wind always be at your back.
> May the rain fall softly on your fields.
> And until we meet again, may God hold you in the
>   hollow of his hand.

During the month of March, you and your grandchildren can see who can find the most blessings. You could even send them on postcards.

If you have a gift for storytelling, incorporate facts about Ireland into an Irish tale and share it with your grandchildren. Staple several sheets of paper together, typing or writing in your text. Let the grandchildren illustrate the story. If this is not your field of expertise, by all means visit your local library. There you will discover many storybooks filled with Irish tales.

March is also a good month to learn about the hearty potato. Research the potato famine that occurred in Ireland and discover how it affected the Irish. Mail your grandchildren some washable paints and art paper. Then have Mom slice some potatoes in half for potato prints. Your grandchildren can dip the halves into the paint and make prints on the paper. Be sure to tell them to use a different potato for each color of paint and to let one color dry before adding another. Ask your grandchildren to mail you a print for your refrigerator door.

You could also make a video production showing how potatoes grow. Explain that those little, white squiggly things growing out of the potato are buds, or shoots, and are called eyes. Show your grandchildren how to plant a potato. If you have ever grown potatoes in a garden or harvested them, tell your grandchildren about your experiences. Too often we forget that today's generation may only be familiar with instant potatoes in various forms. When I was a child, I had a friend whose mother actually made her own potato chips. Even in my day, that was phenomenal. I was impressed! Discuss which is healthier—instant potatoes out of a box or the real thing. Is there any difference? Why have people switched to instant potatoes?

Have your grandchildren list all the different ways they can think of to fix potatoes. Then invite your children and grandchildren to wind up their potato research with this grand finale. Have the whole family pitch in and make Grandma's potato stew. This stew is perfect for today's busy family because it can be prepared in the most wonderful invention known to modern woman—the slow cooker. Ingredients can be prepared the night before, then placed in a Crock-Pot before going off to work and school. Voilà, instant supper! It will truly be an Irish blessing awaiting your extended family at day's end.

Grandma's Potato Stew

1 pound of cubed beef	salt and pepper
2 cups of water	potatoes, carrots, onion, and celery

Place the stew meat in the bottom of the Crock-Pot. Sprinkle with salt and pepper. Add diced vegetables, then water. The Crock-Pot should be about half full. Cook on low for approximately ten to twelve hours. Tasty!

Weather Watching

March is an opportune time to correspond with your grandchildren about the weather and to become weather-wise. Tune in to the national weather channel on TV, use the internet, or read the daily paper to chart the weather for you and your grandchildren's state and local area. Older grandchildren can participate in weather research. A few suggestions are:

Describe a tornado and explain how it forms.
Describe a hurricane and explain how it forms.
Contrast the two and explain which is common to your state.
Describe the safety procedures to follow in regard to tornadoes and hurricanes.
Describe different types of clouds and explain how they are formed.

Visit the library and check out books about weather. Choose some experiments on the water cycle or creating a rainbow. Be creative, and think of weather topics pertinent to your area. You might even want to make a videotape showing your weather experiment. Mail the tape to your grandchildren and have them videotape their experiment. Each year add experiments to the tape. The tape will be a wonderful keepsake.

Too time consuming? You don't have access to a camcorder? Send weather clippings from your local paper and have your grandchildren do likewise. Chart the temperatures and weather conditions for both areas on a calendar.

Perhaps you and your grandchildren have the availability of a fax machine. If so, you have the perfect way to share the weather. During the month of March exchange daily weather reports. I always feel better knowing what weather is in store for the area where my children and grandchildren live.

Younger grandchildren can participate in the weather watch too. Send them a small notebook or staple a week's worth of blank sheets together. Each day have them draw a picture of the weather. Mom can help them mail it back to you. Better yet, help Mom out by providing a return envelope and postage in your original mailing.

When the day is picture-perfect and the clouds are too, read Charles Shaw's *It Looked Like Spilt Milk* (Harper). This is a great book to read on videotape because the illustrations add to the text.

Shoe boxes make great mailing boxes, so save one for this project. Along with the tape and book, include some white chalk, cotton balls, glue, and blue construction paper. Suggest that the grandchildren take Mom and Dad outside and do some cloud watching. The kids can make pictures of what they think the clouds look like. Perhaps they will mail you one for your refrigerator door. Grandchildren age five through eight will enjoy this book. But I'm a little older, and I love it too!

Marshmallow clouds are a tasty way to wind up this project. Send a note to Mom asking her to purchase some saltine crackers and a bag of marshmallows. If you try to mail these items, they might arrive in a crumbly, sticky mess, resembling anything but a cloud.

Marshmallow Clouds

Marshmallows   Saltine crackers

Place individual saltine crackers in a glass baking dish and put a marshmallow on each saltine square. Place the dish in the microwave for
twenty seconds. The marshmallows will puff up like clouds. Be careful! Let them cool. They're yummy!

Windy-Day Activities

The possibilities for this windy month are limitless.
Boys and girls alike will thrill to get outside, especially
if they have been in a wintry climate. Purchase books
about paper airplane flying or buy an airplane kit. Mail
them in time for the first day of spring. Better yet, send
a "windy spring" gift certificate for each grandchild.
Let them make a selection at their local toy store. You
won't be able to go with them, but they'll know where
the gift came from. They'll be thinking of you and will
be excited to tell you about their purchases.

Now it's time for Grandpa to get involved. If he
doesn't enjoy letter writing, he can make a videotape
or cassette tape telling about his kite flying days. Explain how twigs, newspapers, string, and flour-water
paste once were used to make kites that reached high
up in the sky. Be sure to give directions for making the
"just right" kite tail.

Grandma can get in on the act too. Teach the little
ones how to make a pinwheel out of paper. Measure
and cut an 8 1/2 x 11-inch sheet of paper to form an 8
1/2-inch square. Lay a ruler diagonally across the
square. Mark a 5 1/2-inch line in from each corner. Cut
on each line and fold every other flap to the center.

Insert a paper fastener, or brad, through the center to secure the flaps. (Brads may be purchased where office supplies are sold.) A drinking straw can be used as a pinwheel stick. Make vertical slits (near the top) through both sides of the straw. Push the ends of the brad through the slits; then open the ends of the brad. Grandchildren may want to color their paper with unique designs before forming it into a pinwheel. Tell how much pinwheels cost when you were a little girl and compare that to today's cost.

You may also want to send supplies for making a windsock. Little ones will appreciate construction paper, child-safe scissors, crepe paper, and glue sticks. Older grandchildren will have more fun creating with fabrics. To make a windsock, use a sheet of construction paper to form a cylinder, and glue or staple it. Attach twelve-inch crepe paper streamers, approximately two inches apart, around one end of the cylinder. This will be the bottom of the windsock. Punch two holes directly across from each other at the top of the cylinder. Thread a twelve-inch piece of string or yarn through the holes for hanging. Older children may want to use fabric strips for their streamers.

Another way to set the stage for this windy month is to mail your grandchildren a videotape of *The Wizard of Oz*. What a fun way to spend an afternoon—snuggled in a chair watching Dorothy and her friends. A coloring book on this classic along with a new box of crayons will add the perfect touch. If you have an old pair of red shoes, and a granddaughter who would be enchanted with them, then by all means mail them to her. You might even find a pair of red shoes in your granddaughter's size. What fun she can have clicking her heels together pretending to be Dorothy.

Windy-day books are also fun. *Buster's Blustery Day* by Hisako Madokoro, with English text by Patricia Lantier (Gareth Stevens Children's Books), is a story about a windy day and a puppy. *The Turnaround Wind* by Arnold Lobel (Harper & Row) is about a sudden wind that turns the day topsy-turvy. The illustrations are fun. You can view one scene when the book is upright and another scene when the book is upside down. Richard Scarry's *Be Careful, Mr. Frumble* (Random House) is filled with colorful pictures to delight the younger children. *Wind* by Jason Cooper (Rourke Corporation) contains many educational facts about the wind and is written in an easy to understand format.

Celebrate Spring

When the earth awakens after a long winter's sleep and crayon-bright buds burst forth, it's time to celebrate. My heart thrills when the spring flowers begin to poke their heads up to say hello. Challenge your grandchildren to adopt a tree, a clump of flowers, or a patch of grass for a spring watch. Grandpa and Grandma need to choose an area at home to observe too.

Send an outdoor one-time-use camera for this project. Have your grandchildren take snapshots as they begin their watch. Each day, grandchildren and grandparents should check the area for signs of growth—new buds or brighter greens—then record their findings. A miniature notebook is useful for this task. Remind your grandchildren to take pictures whenever they notice a change, especially when their adopted area is in full spring finery. Exchange the notes and the photos by mail.

Hand-sized photo albums are ideal for storing these photos and notes. Inexpensive and colorful, they are a nice extra to include with this project. Be sure to have your grandchildren write their names and the year of their spring watch on the inside of the album.

This activity will teach them to observe the miracles of God as they unfold before their eyes. I have lived through many springs. Yet, I am always amazed when spring slips in quickly. I think I'm watching every minute, but if I turn my head, she dons her new garment in an instant. The brown tones of winter change almost undetected to glimmers of green. Every year I determine to observe more carefully.

It's also time to snap that spring photo for the postcard collection. Try catching Grandpa as he mows the lawn or washes his truck. Perhaps you'll be fortunate enough to capture the first round of flowers as they burst into bloom, accenting your home.

Dr. Seuss's Birthday

Guess who's having a birthday? Dr. Seuss. It's the perfect time and the perfect month to read the book *Green Eggs and Ham* (Random House). After all, everything is turning green. Have Grandpa videotape you stirring up his breakfast. What will you serve? Why, green eggs and ham, of course! Again, these items are impossible to mail, so enlist help from Mom and Dad in providing these delicacies for your grandchildren. Don't forget to praise everyone for their courageous spirit.

You might want to read several Dr. Seuss books on tape. Be sure to send along some birthday hats for this occasion. Your grandchildren will love wearing the party hats as they listen to Grandpa or Grandma read to them.

Before I leave this section on March, I want to make a suggestion. You may want to consider videotaping several books on one tape. If you do this for each month of the year, your grandchildren will have a very unique library. What a legacy this would be. Get Grandpa involved too! Just think, generations from now your grandchild might be saying, "This was Grandpa and Grandma so and so." You could even include Bible stories. What a heritage! "For you have heard my vows, O God; you have given me the heritage of those who fear your name" (Ps. 61:5).

March on in your endeavor to grandparent by long distance!

Journaling Pages

    While unfastening our two-year-old grandson's car seat,
I said, "Stand up!"
    He promptly replied, "Stand up for Jesus!"

Wait 'til you hear what my grandchild said . . .

Here's a bright idea for long-distance grandparenting . . .

Name of grandchild

Long-distance activity

Date completed

Name of grandchild

Long-distance activity

Date completed

Name of grandchild

Long-distance activity

Date completed

Name of grandchild

Long-distance activity

Date completed

April

Spring pastels abound in yards blooming with daffodils and tulips. It is the season of new life. The drama continues to unfold in flower beds throughout the land and on farms in the rural countryside. Your family may even be excitedly awaiting the birth of new pets. What a wonderful time to celebrate the resurrection of our Savior and the new life that Christ enables us to have.

Easter

Easter sometimes falls in March and sometimes in April. In A.D. 325, the Council of Nicaea settled the dispute as to when Easter would occur. They declared that the celebration would take place on the first Sunday after the March 21 full moon. If the full moon occurs on a Sunday, Easter is set for the next Sunday. The Easter celebration never occurs before March 22 or after April 25.

Easter is a celebration commemorating the resurrection of our Lord and Savior, Jesus Christ. The celebration's name in Greek, French, and other Roman languages is taken from the Hebrew *Pesach,* meaning Passover. However, the English name comes from the Anglo-Saxon *Eostre,* an April festival celebrating the goddess of light, or spring. (Information taken from the *Holy Bible* © 1958 by the John A. Hertel Co.)

Easter Crafts

When I was a little girl, I was told we wore new clothes on Easter to symbolize the new life that Christ provides for us. Today many people have lost sight of this reason, but much to the delight of the stores, we have seized the custom.

I remember one Easter dress that was dear to my heart. It was a pastel plaid with puffed sleeves. The skirt had three tiers edged in lace. I felt just like a princess. Every grandma wants her granddaughters to feel the same way. Easter shopping and planning for grandchildren is a grand event. Blessed are the daughters and daughters-in-law who let grandmas participate in a significant way.

Sewing has always been a hobby in our family. My mother sews, I sew, and my daughter sews. My granddaughters are fortunate to have a great-grandma, a grandma, and a mom sewing up seams with dreams. Today there is such a wide selection of fabric designs available, and they are so adorable. Grandma's heart will burst with pride as she imagines little Suzie in the dress she fashions with love. Toddler boy clothing can be included in the sewing designs, but I've found that after a certain age, it is better to shop for a boy's Easter attire.

If sewing is not your hobby, find other ways to create Easter memories. Some grandmas crochet or knit. One Easter I knitted Easter bunnies for all the children in our family. My mother has crocheted Easter baskets, little chicks, and other items. A friend makes ceramic Easter eggs to give as keepsakes. Grandpas and grandmas who enjoy working with wood can create all kinds of cute Easter cutouts. Bake some Easter goodies. Write an Easter story, paint a picture, or take a special photograph. Use your God-given talent to make your grandchildren's Easter an event to remember. Again, these may be shared through visits, videos, cassettes, or mail. Work with what you have available.

Easter Eggs

Another symbol of new life is the egg. Every grandparent envisions hosting an annual Easter egg hunt. But there are those miles again, separating us from our grandchildren, making the event an impossibility. What is a grandparent to do? Well, there are several alternatives. You may not be able to visit on Easter, but if you can visit in the spring, then have a before, or after, Easter egg hunt. The grandchildren don't care if it is on the exact date. Perhaps it is their spring break, and they will get to visit you.

If you are the traveler, don't bother purchasing and packing all those plastic eggs and candy. Wait until you arrive at their home, then make a quick shopping trip. Soon you'll be ready to hide the goodies. Fill some of the eggs with coins. The children like them even better than the candy.

When visiting is out of the question, do the next best thing. Fill the plastic eggs, place them in Styrofoam egg cartons, box up the cartons, and mail them. Your adult children will be glad to hide the eggs for you and may even make a videotape of the fun. If a video is out of the question, you'll probably receive a phone call or letter telling you how many eggs they found. Your grandchildren will know this hunt is hosted by their grandparents. They will treasure the memory.

When you're packing for a visit or packing supplies to mail, include an Easter egg coloring kit. Write on a recipe card the directions for boiling eggs. I'm sure their mom can assist them, but they can add this card to their recipe box. If you feel like being creative, make a videotape of you coloring eggs. You can't mail boiled eggs of course, but you don't have to waste them. I'll bet your church or community would appreciate having them for their hunt.

You can also use eggs to teach your grandchildren the biblical message of Easter. Buy a dozen plastic eggs and number the outside of the eggs 1 to 12. Write the twelve Scripture references (below) on small pieces of paper. Fill each egg with the corresponding verse and small object listed.

1. cotton ball sprayed with perfume; Matthew 26:6–13
2. dime; Matthew 26:14–16
3. bread crust; Matthew 26:17–29
4. olive (in plastic wrap); Matthew 26:30, 36–46
5. piece of paper with a lipstick kiss on it; Matthew 26:47–68
6. small, dried chicken bone; Matthew 26:31–35, 69–75
7. piece of string or yarn and a clod of dirt; Matthew 27:1–10
8. piece of red cloth; Matthew 27:11–31

9. cross (two twigs tied with dental floss to form the shape of a cross) and two nails; Matthew 27:32–44
10. piece of a sponge; Matthew 27:45–56
11. rock or marble; Matthew 27:57–65
12. nothing; Matthew 28:1–8

Have your grandchildren place the eggs in a carton on their dining room table or wherever their family meets. Twelve days before Easter, they should open the first egg and find the Scripture passage in the Bible and read it. Tell them to open one egg a day in order through Easter Sunday. Hearts will overflow with the newness of life from these eggs.

Easter Dinner

When I was growing up, Easter dinner was always a grand affair. My grandma was a terrific cook. My mom still carries on the tradition. But if some members of the family can't make it home, why not share some of Grandma's recipes. We usually have ham and turkey on Easter. The latter is so we can have broth with Grandma's noodles. I'm sure you have your own traditional dishes that you prepare for Easter. If not, here's our noodle recipe. Share it with your children and grandchildren who can't be home this Easter. Both of you roll up a batch, then enjoy!

Homemade Noodles

1 egg	2 tbsp milk
1/2 tsp salt	1 cup of flour

Beat together the egg, salt, and milk. Add the flour. Roll out the dough as thin as possible on a floured surface. Cut the dough into rectangular shapes, stack, and slice into noodles. (I use a pizza cutter. It works great!) The noodles may be made twenty minutes ahead of time or the night before. Unused noodles may be frozen. This recipe will serve about three to four people, so you will need to multiply it depending on the size of your family.

If you are cooking noodles for eight to ten people, you will need a pan large enough to hold five or six quarts of broth. Add one teaspoon of salt to the broth to begin with (more may be added later if necessary). If you are using canned broth, check to see whether salt has already been added. When using rich broth from a hen or turkey, you may add up to a quart of water to increase the amount of broth.

Heat your broth to a rolling boil. Drop in the noodles a few at a time, keeping the broth boiling. Turn the heat down to medium and continue stirring frequently. Boil the noodles for ten minutes. Reduce the heat to low and simmer for another five to ten minutes until the noodles are tender. Don't be concerned about the extra flour on the noodles. It will thicken the broth, making the noodles nice and creamy.

Rainy-Day Activities

Showers are sure to share center stage with the sun and the wind this month. Rest assured that the rain is playing a big part in the spring production.

Care Packages

Prepare a care package for those rainy days that keep your grandchildren indoors. Send brightly colored markers, new crayons, coloring books, and sketch pads.

You may also want to send a craft care package. You don't have to purchase all the items for a craft project. Instead, look around your home for craft materials: old necklaces or beads (if your grandchildren are old enough to use these items), Styrofoam trays and containers from the grocery deli, cotton balls, colorful craft chenille sticks, glue, and fabric scraps from Grandma's sewing box or small wood scraps and sandpaper from Grandpa. Again, make sure the supplies are age appropriate. Mom will not be pleased if the children sand her furniture. Package all the rainy-day supplies in a plastic box for easy storage.

Videos and Books

Mail a video version of *Mary Poppins* for rainy day viewing, or select your own favorite. Along with the *Mary Poppins* video, send umbrellas. Many umbrellas are designed to be very compact and are easily mailed. I can guarantee that the grandchildren will be thrilled to have their own rain gear. I've had firsthand experience!

A visit to the bookstore, or library, will provide you with many ideas for April books. *Peter Rabbit* by Beatrix Potter (Publications International), *The Velveteen Rabbit* by Margery Williams (Avon Camelot), and *Frog and Toad Are Friends* by Arnold Lobel (Scholastic) are among the many. A beautiful book that teaches about sharing is *The Rainbow Fish* by Marcus Pfister (North-South Books). Browse, browse, browse among the bookshelves. Then read, read, read and prepare a cassette or videotape for those precious little ones. Don't forget to send some books of fiction for the older grandchildren. You might want to start them on a series. That way you can add to their collection each month.

There are four benefits to sharing books with your grandchildren: (1) Book sharing can fit any budget; (2) book sharing can fit any time schedule; (3) children love books; (4) you can employ a variety of methods for your shared reading.

Reading books to your grandchildren can be as expensive or as inexpensive as you want it to be. Libraries enable us to have access to the best. If your budget allows, then by all means, it is money wisely spent when you add to your grandchildren's personal library. But the important point is that a special bonding occurs when grandparents and grandchildren share books.

Noah's Ark

Since this is the month of April showers, don't forget to share the story of Noah's ark. There are many versions of this book on the market for younger grandchildren. Share the story right from God's Word with the older grandchildren. Be sure to point out Genesis 2:5–6. Noah's faith appears even greater when we consider that up until the time he entered the ark it had never rained. All sorts of novelty items are available for purchase, such as a replica of the ark and animals, jewelry, tea sets, music boxes, key rings, coloring books, and so on. You can even do a craft project, creating the ark and animals out of boxes and clay.

Promise Books and Letters

Whenever I think of Noah, I think of rainbows. Whenever I think of rainbows, I think of God's promises. When rainy days are clouding up the hope of all ages, present your grandchildren with their very own copy of a promise book. These can be purchased in most Christian bookstores and contain promise references for specific times. They are handy to have and present key verses for easy memorization.

You may also want to start a promise letter. When you find a promise in God's Word that especially speaks to you, write a letter to your grandchildren claiming the verse as a promise. Then have them add a promise that they have discovered and mail the letter back to you. This continues until you have a collection of promise verses. You can buy file cards that are spiral bound. These little books would be perfect for this activity. If you have several grandchildren who are old enough to do this project, have them select topics and find key verses on their topics. Remember, tailor your grandparenting activities to fit your family.

The promise of Easter can be found in every rainbow!

Journaling Pages

I was outside with our two-year-old grandson when he asked, "Grandma, do you have a ladder?"

"Why do you need one?" I questioned.

"I want to climb up and talk to God."

"You don't have to climb up to God, just close your eyes and talk to him."

Closing his eyes, the little guy said, "Hi, God!"

Wait 'til you hear what my grandchild said . . .

_____

_____

_____

_____

_____

_____

_____

Here's a bright idea for long-distance grandparenting . . .

_____

_____

_____

_____

_____

_____

_____

_____

Name of grandchild

Long-distance activity

Date completed

Name of grandchild

Long-distance activity

Date completed

Name of grandchild

Long-distance activity

Date completed

Name of grandchild

Long-distance activity

Date completed

May

Spring is in her glory! She's all dressed up in her finest as if awaiting prom night.

In Indiana, the redbuds, dogwoods, and lilacs are creating picture postcard settings. Even if your spring peaked earlier, it's still a grand month for celebrating spring.

Proms, graduations, end-of-school programs, Mother's Day, Memorial Day, baseball, softball, and planting season all provide us with many opportunities to grandparent by long distance. Get the pad and pen, turn on the fax, e-mail, dial the phone, get out the camcorder or cassette player, or take some snapshots. The choice is yours—how will you be a part of these important moments in your grandchild's life?

Dress-up Events

There is something enchanting about the month of May. Spring isn't the only one who wants to dress up in her finery. So put on the frilliest dresses and the classiest of suits and have an old-fashioned Victorian tea party. During one of my grandchildren's visits, I took them to a tea room. It was such a memorable time that the next spring we held our own tea. Yes, we dressed up for the occasion. A little grandeur helps set the mood. Sometimes, I get a yearning to recapture these story-book moments, but my grandchildren live so far away.

My friend Margaret Anne Huffman gave me the answer in her book, *Everyday Prayers for Grandmothers* (Dimensions for Living). Margaret Anne mentioned that she had bought two matching tea sets and mailed one to her granddaughter. Perfect! Excitedly, I went shopping and was fortunate enough to find two tea sets that match my dishes. You can even take it further. When you are mailing your tea set, include some fancy napkins, Scripture tea bags, and dainty cookies. Your grandchildren will love all the splendor.

Little girls who dream of being Cinderella and waltzing off to the ball soon grow up and dance the night away at the high school prom. Whether your grandchildren are as beautiful as Cinderella or as charming as the Prince, you want to be a part of their enchanted evening. Persuade Mom and Dad to capture the evening on videotape or snap enough photographs to fill a volume of Grandma's brag book. The key to long-distance grandparenting is sharing a part of yourself. Grandparents, recall your first prom. Share the story on cassette tape or by letter. Photocopy your prom pictures and mail them to your grandchildren. They will be delighted to see how styles have changed. Perhaps the styles have come full circle.

Springtime Care Package

Sunny days are here again, and it's time to send a care package. The miles may prevent you from kissing those hurts or skinned knees, but you can do the next best thing—choose some colorful Band-Aids, the kind that Mom seldom buys. After all, grandchildren are for spoiling. Pack some sunglasses to shield those little eyes and include some suntan lotion to protect their delicate skin from the first sunny rays. It's also fun to include sun visors and caps, along with sandals. If you're not sure of sizes, send gift certificates for sandals or summer play clothes. Springtime is also the ideal time to send money for ice cream treats. Don't attempt to send everything I've mentioned. The idea is to let your grandchildren know you are anticipating with them the joy of sunny days. Keep your care package small and simple. Use a different idea each year.

Gardening Fun

Gardening anyone? In Indiana, May is planting time. One spring my grandchildren were visiting, and they helped me pot the flowers for the patio. We ended up with more dirt on us than in the pots, but it was fun. I remember another time when the two oldest grandchildren were quite small. They wanted to help me weed and started to reach for the greenery. Quickly, I said, "Oh, no! I'll have to do it. You might pull up the plants with the weeds." Immediately, I thought of the parable of the weeds that Jesus shared in Matthew 13:24–30.

Then the little ones asked a very important question. "But, Grandma, how do we know the difference between the weeds and the plants?"

I muttered that in time they would learn to recognize which were plants and which were weeds. Dusk was falling and there wasn't time to begin the lesson. Gardening experience has taught them to recognize the difference between many plants and weeds. In the same way, their spiritual experiences are teaching them to discern between things of God and things of the world.

Gardening, or planting, must be very near to the heart of God, for Jesus told many parables about the sower, seeds, plants, and harvesting. As a gardener or farmer goes about planting and harvesting tasks, the parables of Christ come alive with meaning. Begin to cultivate within your grandchildren a love and respect for the cycle of planting, nourishing, and harvesting.

Send small inexpensive gardening tools along with seed packets and gardening gloves. I suggest you include some pumpkin seeds. They are almost always successful, and you can use pumpkins for projects in the fall. Books on square-foot gardening can provide how-to information. Square-foot gardening is ideal when there is little space.

When you mail your gardening tools and seeds, include the ingredients and the directions for making this earthy treat. If your grandchildren are small, you'll have to enlist Mom's help. Older grandchildren will be able to create this down-to-earth surprise for the family.

A Down-to-Earth Surprise

1 package of instant vanilla pudding   1 package of Gummi Worms
1 package of chocolate cookies

Mix the pudding according to the directions on the box. Pour into dessert cups. Hide a Gummi Worm in the pudding. Crush the cookies by placing them between wax paper, then rolling with a rolling pin, or smash cookies with the bottom of a plastic glass. Sprinkle the crumbs on top of the pudding to look like dirt. Watch the eyes of family members as they discover their hidden surprises.

Tissue Flowers

I remember making tissue flowers when I was a child. In my day, tissues were always white. Sometimes we would take a crayon and color the tips of the flowers. They always reminded me of carnations. We would pin them in our hair or fashion a construction paper May basket to share with someone special.

As a grandmother, and a teacher, I always marvel to see the delight on children's faces when they first learn to make tissue flowers. Something simple brings much joy. Packages of pink, yellow, and blue tissues can provide hours of fun while also providing a bountiful garden of blossoms. This is a joyful project that costs relatively little.

In case you missed out on learning how to make tissue flowers, I have listed the steps below:

1. Open the tissue into its full rectangular shape.
2. Fold in half, then once again. It should be folded in fourths now.
3. Trim narrowly along the folded edges with scissors.
4. Gather in the middle and secure tightly with a pipe cleaner or hair pin.
5. Gently pick tissue sheets apart, lifting upward toward the center.
6. Presto! You have just created a blossom.

Package some colorful packages of tissues, pipe cleaners or hair pins, child-safe scissors, construction paper, glue, and tape. I suggest you make a videotape demonstrating this craft. If that isn't possible, mail the directions to Mom. She may even have made them in her youth. Be sure to send samples of a work in progress, plus a completed flower. The directions will serve to refresh her memory. Since they won't have a grandma to surprise with a May basket, let them choose (with Mom's guidance) a neighbor, friend, or church member who would enjoy receiving one.

Mother's Day

Special! That's how you want Mom to feel on Mother's Day. Encourage your grandchildren to pamper her. How they do it depends on their ages. If they are old enough, they can serve her breakfast in bed, complete with fresh flowers from the great outdoors. It doesn't matter if the flowers are golden dandelions or miniature violets. Wildflowers are beautiful, and Mom will treasure a gift from the heart.

Suggest that the children allow Mom one golden hour of peace. During that hour, no one interrupts her, unless, of course, there is a major crisis and Dad isn't around to handle it. Motivate your grandchildren to think of other ways to pamper their mom.

Grandparents, plant the seeds of thoughtfulness in the hearts of your grandchildren. Encourage them to make cards by writing expressions of their love and appreciation to their mom. Tucked away in my closet are cards and letters that my children made for me on Mother's Day. Every once in a while, I happen upon them. Lovingly, I unfold them, rereading and reminiscing. These are heart gifts that money can't buy.

Among my prized possessions is a note from one of my granddaughters. It simply reads, "To Grandma, I love you." She surrounded her sentiment with a garden of pastel flowers and placed it in a frame that she purchased with her own money. Precious! In fact, I have a growing collection of hand-crafted items that my grandchildren have given me for Mother's Day, birthdays, Christmas, and "just because." The love that prompted the crafting is what makes each gift special.

When it comes to Mother's Day, purchased gifts may be given in addition to some thoughtful act of pampering. Advise your grandchildren to put time and thought into their gift selections. A thoughtful gift considers Mom's personality. What type of gift would she appreciate? Some moms love fresh cut flowers; others see them as a waste. Some moms are thrilled to receive a gift certificate, while others think you've taken the easy way out. Know your mom! Grandma, here's your chance to help make Mother's Day extra special for both the giver and the receiver.

Memorial Day

Memorial Day falls on the last Monday of the month. Many children do not know the reason for this holiday. Grandparents, share some family history. Recall how you spent Memorial Day as a child.

Early in the morning we gathered fresh flowers from the yard and put them in quart jars or tin cans with foil. We had as many as ten bunches. Then we set off, with Daddy driving the entire family to the cemetery. There we bestowed our fresh cuttings of peonies and irises on the graves of our beloved ancestors. Our parents always told us stories about Aunt Sally or Uncle Jim. We listened attentively as our parents traveled backward in time, reliving a little bit of their childhoods. Of course, if there was a war veteran in the family, that grave received special honors. Miniature American flags spoke of the courage of the person buried there. After hearing about our own families, we walked about, listening as Mom and Dad talked of neighbors and friends from the past.

The tradition of bridging generations through oral history and instilling respect for those who have gone before helped build our character. As our parents spoke of our ancestors in revered tones, we were challenged to live up to our family's expectations. We learned not to be afraid of death and to respect the graves of our ancestors. We understood that only the shells of their earthly lives remained in the graves, and that their souls lived on in the hereafter.

After our visit to the cemetery, we returned home and had a family picnic. Each relative brought something so that no one person had to work too hard. A radio blared in the background as the adults listened to the Indy 500. Ball games were played, and horseshoes were pitched. Adults and children played together. In the evening, the kids caught fireflies and placed them in jars or glass pop bottles to make lanterns.

Today we seldom visit cemeteries. Holidays such as Thanksgiving, Christmas, and Easter may be the only time families can get together. The tradition of visiting hallowed graves is past, but the oral tradition of keeping ancestral memories alive can be carried on in a different manner. Prepare a tape in time for Memorial Day. Explain the meaning of the day and why it was established. Then tell how you spent Memorial Day as a child.

Now may also be the time to fill a photo album with genealogical information about grandparents, aunts, and uncles. Make family history come alive for your grandchildren. Carry the thread from one generation to the next, stitching together your family. Make a new Memorial Day tradition.

Outdoor Activities

Grandpa, fishing is a little difficult by long distance, but do what you can. Get Dad involved. Artificial lures are easily mailed. A gift certificate for a new fishing pole will be appreciated, so will sharing those fish tales. Get out the cassette recorder and tell a few stories. When you land a "big one," mail a photo of your catch. Place your snapshot in a talking photo and record a message.

Baseball and softball season is here. Have Mom and Dad videotape the grandchildren's games or send some snapshots. Share information about favorite teams within your state. Record stories about your ball playing days.

Chances are, you can find toy replicas of your favorite hobby or sport to share with the little tykes. Miniature golfing sets, fishing poles, and batting sets are just a few examples. If they're too cumbersome to mail, gift certificates are the answer for these inexpensive summer toys.

Springtime on the Farm

Many times Grandpa and Grandma live in a rural area. Maybe they're still on the farm.

Mom and Dad went off to college, received college degrees, and moved to the city to find a job in their field of education. If that is the case, then don't miss the opportunity to share the wonders of rural living, and vice versa.

In the spring when new life abounds with the birth of farm animals, videotape the playful animals, from baby calves to baby kittens. Capture the farmers plowing the fields and planting the seeds. Miniature toy tractors and plastic farm animals are inexpensive purchases that will brighten a small grandchild's eyes.

Ask your grandchildren to tell you about life where they live. Where do they go? What do they play? Have them describe the view from their window. Exchange and compare your daily routines. Introduce the books *The Town Mouse and the Country Mouse* by Helen Craig (Candlewick Press) and *Charlotte's Web* by E. B. White (Harper & Row) to your younger grandchildren.

Books and Activities

When you set up the camcorder or plug in the cassette recorder to read to your grandchildren, share a few memories. The older grandchildren especially love hearing these tales. But let me repeat my motto for long-distance grandparenting: Tell the tales that might not get told unless you take the time to tell them!

Have you ever gone barefoot in the spring? Tell your grandchildren about the first time. Did the grass tickle your toes? Children today, for numerous reasons, seldom go barefoot. Maybe it's because they're on the go, live in a city, or have lots of sandals. Were there hon-

eybees where you lived? Did you ever step on one?
What did you do? Introduce Eric Carle's moving picture book *The Honeybee and the Robber* (Scholastic).

Are You My Mother? by P. D. Eastman (Random
House) is a fun book for spring. It's about a little bird
who has gotten separated from his mother and is
searching for her. This book provides an opportunity
for Grandpa to get involved and demonstrate how to
make some birdhouses. You can find directions at the
library or in magazines. Pop bottles and milk cartons
are among the items that can be used. If Grandpa is
good at woodworking, maybe he can cut the wood and
mail it. Your grandchildren could then assemble it with
glue or nails depending on their ages. If this isn't fea-
sible due to time or age, you can purchase inexpensive bird feeders for hummingbirds and other birds.
Send a book that shows and tells about several different types of birds. Have your grandchildren keep a
record of the birds they spot. This is also a good time
to send a recipe for some tasty bird nest treats.

Tasty Bird Nests

1 can of chow mein noodles	1 package of jelly beans (minia-
1 package of butterscotch	ture, if you can find them)
morsels	

Place the butterscotch morsels in a glass baking dish and melt them in
the microwave for three to five minutes. Stir in the noodles, coating
them. Quickly form the mixture into round nests, denting in the center. Add some jelly beans and presto—a neat, nesty snack!

May is a timely month to read *Mother's Day Mice* by
Eve Bunting (Clarion Books), as well as *Blueberries for*

Sal by Robert McCloskey (Puffin Books). Ever go berry pickin'? Tell your grandchildren about it. What kind of berries did you pick? Raspberries, blackberries, blueberries, or strawberries? Did you eat more than you brought back? What did you put the berries in? What did your family do with the berries? Chances are they made jams and jellies—this is almost a lost art due to our busy schedules.

If you are making a videotape, you may want to make some jam. Even if the berries in your or your grandchildren's geographical region are not ripe, fresh berries are available at the supermarket. Place a batch of your jam or jelly in a plastic jar, package carefully, and mail. They'll think of you when they enjoy it on their morning toast. Or you can mail your grandchildren some Sure-Jell, and with Mom's help they can stir up a batch of their own.

If making jams and jellies is out of the question, buy some little jars of gourmet jelly. The grandchildren will love sampling the different varieties. You'll still be sending "love from Grandma," while keeping it fast, simple, and easy!

Little Red Hen is an ageless story that still teaches about doing your share of the work. Mom will love you for reminding her crew members to pull their own weight. The story also fits nicely with planting season. I can almost smell the aroma of homemade bread baking. Bread making and bread baking are among my fondest memories of visiting Grandma. There is nothing more yummy than melted home churned butter on a steamy yeast roll. My mother continued this tradition. Many days I would return home from school to the smell of yeast rolls. Heavenly!

As I entered the work force, and time became a factor, this tradition got pushed by the wayside. Fortunately, bread makers and frozen bread dough supply us with the real scent and almost the real taste. But I challenge you to get out your recipe books and stir up a batch of bread from scratch. Videotape yourself reading *The Little Red Hen,* then demonstrate bread baking. Mailing bread is probably out of the question, but send the recipe. Maybe Mom will have some extra time, and they can whip up a batch of their own. The point is they will see Grandma baking bread.

You might even want to wait until your grandchildren are visiting or you're visiting them to do your bread making. My oldest grandchildren participated in a bread making event while Great-Grandma and Grandma (me) visited. The grandchildren, ages eleven, nine, and six, stirred up their own batches of bread. Next, even the two-year-old joined in the fun. All four grandchildren kneaded, baked, and shared their final products. The afternoon was a memorable one for us all. I might warn you, the experience may turn your hair white. After all, flour seems to go everywhere. Now, what did you think I meant?

Happy baking and jamming with your grandchildren!

Journaling Pages

I had bought our young granddaughter some play money and play groceries. A couple of days later, we were shopping. She had left her real money at home. I told her I'd lend her some money and she could pay me back later. As we were leaving the store, she said, "Grandma, I don't suppose it'd be right—no, it wouldn't."

"What, sweetheart?" I asked.

"I was going to pay you with that fake money."

Wait 'til you hear what my grandchild said . . .

_____

_____

_____

_____

_____

_____

Here's a bright idea for long-distance grandparenting . . .

_____

_____

_____

_____

_____

_____

Name of grandchild

Long-distance activity

Date completed

Name of grandchild

Long-distance activity

Date completed

Name of grandchild

Long-distance activity

Date completed

Name of grandchild

Long-distance activity

Date completed

June

une—spring bows out and summer sweeps
in. Branches laden with gracious, green leaves
prance in summer's premier, inviting us to
have a picnic.

Summer Picnic

A picnic basket might be a little cumbersome to
mail, but you can pack a smaller box with plastic forks,
plates, napkins, and a tablecloth with a picnic design.
Add a package containing a cool summer drink mix
and a box of teddy bear cookies.

You might suggest that your grandchildren make
peanut butter and jelly sandwiches. Include a bread
press that imprints the words "Have a Nice Day" onto
the bread slices. Your grandchildren will have a great
time imprinting their sandwiches. A press can be purchased from various party lines and novelty stores.
The little ones can easily put together this picnic
snack. A carefree Mom may decide to expand the menu
and join the youngsters. If she's busy, she'll thank you
for this simplistic bundle. One other thing—be sure to
tell your grandchildren to invite their teddy bears, for

this is the teddy bears' picnic. You might even want to send a sing-along tape of the song "The Teddy Bears' Picnic" (Warner Brothers) or the book *The Teddy Bears' Picnic* by Jimmy Kennedy, illustrated by Prue Theobalds (Peter Bedrick Books).

Story Time

Eric Carle, a renowned children's author, celebrates his birthday on June 25. *Brown Bear, Brown Bear, What Do You See?* (Henry Holt & Co.) is a delightful book that he illustrated. Another is *Polar Bear, Polar Bear, What Do You Hear?* (Scholastic). The verses for both books were written by Bill Martin Jr. Children love these sing-song question and answer books.

The Grouchy Ladybug, The Honeybee and the Robber (I mentioned this one in May), *The Very Busy Spider, The Very Quiet Cricket, The Very Hungry Caterpillar,* and *Papa, Please Get the Moon for Me* are all entertaining books by Carle (Scholastic). Mail copies of the books along with a cassette tape. Get Grandpa involved and have him read a book or two. Most of Carle's books come in paperback as well as hardback, but some of the hardback copies will steal your heart. They come with sound effects.

Since June is the month for the teddy bears' picnic, take advantage of all the bear books on the market: A. A. Milne's Winnie the Pooh books, Stan and Jan Berenstain's The Berenstain Bears (Random House), The Little Bear series by Elsie H. Minarik (Harper & Row), plus many others. Don't forget the all-time favorite, *Goldilocks and the Three Bears.*

Graduation

Proms are over and the end of the school year is fast approaching. If you happen to be the proud grandparent of a high school or college senior, it is graduation time! You want to make the milestone special, but the question is how. We tend to think that big events call for big gifts, when, in fact, the more momentous the occasion, the more meaningful the gift should be. Sometimes we get confused and try to say how we feel with dollars and cents.

Graduation is the opportune time for monetary gift giving, especially with the expenses of the future looming on the horizon. Along with the gift of your choice, though, share your life stories, and don't miss the opportunity to pass on an heirloom of significant meaning. Grandma, now may be the time to give that string of pearls or locket that means something special to you. Did Grandpa give it to you? Grandpa, do you have a special key ring or pocketknife?

Share your story. Share yourself. What made your graduation special? What emotions did you feel? Your grandchild is probably experiencing some of the same feelings. What made you decide on your career? Make it a point to tell the stories that may never be told when grandparents and grandchildren live far apart. Personally, I've found the cassette recorder ideal for sharing. Most teenagers have headsets and can listen any time. Don't underestimate today's kids. They want to connect with those who care about them. They'll be glad to have a treasure from their grandparents' lives.

Flag Day

Flag Day arrives on June 14. This holiday doesn't receive the fanfare that other holidays do. Grandparents, here's your chance to plant the seeds of patriotism in young hearts. Gather information about the holiday. When was Flag Day first recognized? Learn the proper care of the United States flag. Research the history of the first American flag. Talk about the meaning of the flag's design. Yes, your grandchildren may have learned this information in school, but it's reminder time.

Mail some American flag stickers or a package of those little paper flags that are often used on cupcakes. Design a family flag, either on paper or with fabric. Grandma, if you're into sewing, be creative with all the red, white, and blue fabrics on the market. Into crafts? Create some American memorabilia: earrings, T-shirts, wooden cutouts—whatever fits your budget, time, and the ages of your grandchildren.

Share the Scripture from 2 Chronicles 7:14: "If my people, who are called by my name, will humble themselves and pray and seek my face and turn from their wicked ways, then will I hear from heaven and will forgive their sin and will heal their land." Challenge them to pray for America and its leaders.

Father's Day

Every June, fathers throughout the land are given special recognition by their children. This celebration gives meaning to the fifth commandment: "Honor your father and your mother" (Exod. 20:12). Grandma, share some ideas with your grandchildren on how they can honor their father. You might suggest they create an "I will help . . ." card, thus giving a part of themselves. The child could give a card agreeing to help Dad with some task. Washing the car is an example.

With Mom's assistance, T-shirts or sweatshirts can be designed for Dad and Grandpa. Mom can guide small hands in and out of paint, pressing colorful handprints onto sweatshirts. Grandchildren can use bottles of squeeze paint to decorate T-shirts with unique designs. These are treasures.

My daughter, along with her children, has created unique gifts by gluing small resin ornaments, magnets, and buttons on men's hats. She searched for items relating to individual personalities. These one-of-a-kind gifts teach children the importance of putting thought and preparation into their gift giving. One little girl summed it up when she said, "Homemade is always best!" The key ingredient is love!

Special Occasions

Weddings, anniversaries, baptisms, piano and dance recitals don't always happen in June, but sometimes they do. Whenever and whatever the special occasion, have someone record it. Share it through a letter, snapshots, cassette tape, or videotape. Our daughter made a priceless tape of our grandchildren from infancy to their present ages. She included Christmas mornings, birthdays, Easters, summer ball games, plus numerous other highlights from their lives. She presented us with this gift for our anniversary. Needless to say, we were thrilled!

Summer Shape-up

Summer time is shape-up time! Today's grandparents are into physical fitness. We want to be healthy and live long, productive lives so we can keep up with our grandchildren. We also know more about the role exercise plays in our lives. We want our children and grandchildren to begin their stretch for physical fitness at an early age. So one, two, three, stretch! Make a videotape of an exercise routine and invite your younger grandchildren to try out the routine with you. If you're not up to having anyone watch you huff and puff, there are some cute exercise videos available. *Sing, Stretch, and Play,* a video by Brentwood Music, includes exercises, Scripture, and songs. This action tape shows adults and young children stretching their bodies, minds, and souls.

Want to accomplish two things at once? Buy a CD or cassette tape of some Christian rock or contemporary music and invite the older grandchildren to walk, jog, or exercise to the music. This will provide them with a Christian message while motivating them to exercise. Health experts tell us that young people today are far too sedentary. In case you're afraid of making the wrong music selections, check out your local Christian bookstores. Some music companies already have exercise tapes on the market.

Stargazing

Summer nights are great for stargazing. Toss a blanket on the ground and check out the night sky. What constellations do you see? Share your information.

Grandparents, here is your chance to teach that God is omnipresent—present everywhere at the same time. Stress that the same stars are shining in the night sky where you and your grandchildren live. The same God is watching over both households and can be present in both locations at the same time. Wow! That fact alone makes a family who is separated by miles feel united. Do a little research before you begin your stargazing. Trips to the library or bookstore are in order.

This is also the ideal time to introduce what the Bible has to say about planning your life by the stars. Isaiah 47:13–15 is a good place to start. Search the Scriptures and find other verses that warn us not to plan our lives by our horoscopes or by what a fortune-teller has to say. Help your grandchildren become grounded in the truth of the Word. Explain the difference between astronomy and astrology. Have your grandchildren look up the two words in the dictionary. Older grandchildren can participate in doing some research at the library. Look for books on this subject in your local Christian bookstores.

Grandma, expand the project. Make some star cookies. Teach the little ones how to draw a star. Mail a package of colored foil stars with some blue or black construction paper. Let them create their own star pictures. Packets of plastic stars that adhere to a ceiling may be purchased. Have Dad and Mom use the stars to form constellations in your grandchildren's bedroom. Write books starring your grandchildren. On each page, draw a star and write a quality that you recognize in your grandchildren. Everyone loves praise, and too often we don't take the time to say it.

Don't miss reading the star book *The Drinking Gourd* by Ferdinand N. Monjo and illustrated by Fred Brenner (HarperCollins). This wonderful story is about the underground railroad and how slaves used the Big Dipper to find their way north to freedom. The story will go perfectly with your stargazing, as well as providing a history lesson.

Share a Hobby

Blessed are the grandmothers and grandfathers who take the time to hand down a skill or craft to their grandchildren. It may be as simple as making lemonade from "real" lemons or stitching quilt squares together. In each family the skills are different, but the blessing is the same—a special bonding between the grandparent and the grandchild.

What skills will you pass on to your grandchild? Grandma, cut those fabric scraps into squares. Mail them along with needle, thread, and a letter explaining what the scraps are from. When my children were little, their great-grandmother taught them to stitch quilt squares together. Later, she gave me a quilt top. What fun we've had reminiscing over the squares: "I remember I had a jumper made out of that one, and you had a dress made out of that fabric." If you have a camcorder available, by all means videotape a demonstration. Little squares can be stitched together in units of four, then mailed back to Grandma. Grandma can stitch them together. A great book to share is *The Patchwork Quilt* by Valerie Flournoy, illustrated by Jerry Pinkney (Dial).

Caring for plants is a learning experience. Perhaps you have a plant that has been in the family for years.

The next time your grandchildren visit, give them a start from the plant and a card explaining how to care for it. Yard plants are great heirlooms to pass on to your children and grandchildren. There is a great deal of comfort in knowing that a flower from Grandma's yard is blooming for the extended family. Dig up some starts from the lilac bush or the plant of your choice and pass it on. If you live in different parts of the country, compare the times when the plants bloom. Which family unit has the earlier spring? Before you transport plants, be sure to check your state laws.

Maybe Grandpa or Grandma is a nature lover. If so, don't let the opportunity slip by to pass on the knowledge that you take for granted. Teach your grandchildren about the different kinds of trees and to watch for the seasonal changes in nature.

Perhaps Grandpa collects arrowheads or butterflies. Maybe he's a sports enthusiast. Does he have a soft spot for animals? The possibilities for sharing a hobby are as limitless as your interests. Remember, whatever your hobby, your grandchildren may share the same interests, for there is a little bit of you in each grandchild.

A Trip down Memory Lane

Grandparents, spin a tale or two about what you did in the summertime. This can be written in letter form or put on a cassette tape. Where did you go and what did you do in the summer? How were things different in your youth? Was it safer? Did you have to worry about strangers bothering you?

What did you do on the weekend? I lived in a farm community and on Saturday night we always went into town. The men sat on benches outside the store and chatted, the women shopped for groceries, and kids of various ages walked around the town with their friends. Does this trigger any memories for you? How did you spend your Sunday? Were the stores open or closed on Sunday? In my day, Sunday was truly a day of rest. Between church services, lazy afternoons were spent with family.

Did your mother work? Did she have certain days for certain household chores? Where did your dad work? The questions could go on and on, but turn on the cassette recorder and talk away. Tell your grandchildren everything you can think of about your youth and everything you can think of about their great-grandparents. They'll listen, enraptured by your tales.

A trip down memory lane can lead to all kinds of exciting possibilities, and they don't have to be expensive. I remember making hollyhock dolls as a child. I doubt that my grandchildren know what hollyhocks are, but I can send them a picture from a seed catalog and write them a story. Better yet, I can mail them some seeds to plant.

The other day I took a walk and saw some morning glories along the roadside. I remembered how these flowers grew along our fence when I was a child. Summer is a wonderful time to get immersed in a study of wildflowers. Purchase a book about wildflowers and mail it to your grandchildren. Let them discover and record the types of wildflowers in their area. You do the same, then exchange information with your grandchildren. Learn how to dry or press flowers. Carry the project one step further and create your own notepaper.

Every life is different. Every tale is woven from different threads. Sometimes we think grandchildren wouldn't be interested in the fabric of our lives. Sometimes they're too busy, and we are too. Perhaps we need to stop and take time to form those family ties into everlasting knots.

Journaling Pages

Our granddaughter, age eight, was playing outside when she accidentally fell backwards into the wading pool—a total surprise. As we were gathering dry clothes, she told me, "When I fell in, I just thought—this has to be a dream!"

Wait 'til you hear what my grandchild said . . .

_____

_____

_____

_____

_____

_____

_____

Here's a bright idea for long-distance grandparenting . . .

_____

_____

_____

_____

_____

_____

_____

_____

Name of grandchild

Long-distance activity

Date completed

Name of grandchild

Long-distance activity

Date completed

Name of grandchild

Long-distance activity

Date completed

Name of grandchild

Long-distance activity

Date completed

July

ardens have been planted, homes have been spruced up, and now it's time to relax. Everyone's thoughts turn to vacation. Who will visit whom and when? Before you begin your trip, bathe it in prayer, asking for God's guidance as you plan and for his protection in travel.

Travel Packages

If the distance between you and your child's family involves several states, help Mom and Dad prepare for the vacation adventure. A few weeks before the planned departure, send a map of the United States so they can chart their trip. Rand McNally for Kids has a set of Backseat Books for children that serve a dual purpose. The series teaches about the states and also keeps grandchildren entertained as they travel the interstate or fly the sky to Grandma's. *Fun Finder, 25 Travel Games* (Rand McNally) is a laminated, fold-up, travel game that comes complete with its own pen.

Headsets are inexpensive and make nice travel gifts. When the miles get long, everyone will need moments to retreat into their own little world. Headsets provide entertainment and offer everyone a reprieve from too much togetherness. You may want to include a favorite tape or two. If you or a friend play the piano, make a tape of the song "Fifty Nifty United States" by Ray Charles (Roncom Music Co.). Your grandchildren will love singing this fun song as they travel to Grandpa and Grandma's.

Small handheld games may be mailed in your travel package, along with a new pad and pen. Recently, I was browsing in a fabric store and happened upon some travel games that were printed on fabric. The fabric brand is called Kidz on the Go. I was thrilled with my discovery. If you are a grandma who likes to sew, here's a unique gift to stitch up. Chronicle Books' Giftworks has a card game entitled *52 Fun Things to Do in the Car* by Lynn Gordon. These packets of cards can be found in bookstores. Of course, if you're feeling creative, invent your own I-spy travel checklist. Compile a list of twenty items. Include places, travel signs, cars and trucks that the children might see along the way. Give each grandchild his or her own list, keeping in mind the age of each child. The list for smaller children may include cows in a field or a McDonald's. Have older grandchildren keep an eye out for a certain model of car or a historical marker.

Through the year, purchase small inexpensive items of interest for your grandchildren. Then when it is time for them to make the long trip to Grandpa and Grandma's, wrap the items individually and mail them. Send a note that says they may open one small gift whenever they enter another state, or designate the gift opening by time or miles. Before you decide on the criteria for opening surprises, consider your grandchild's age, attention span, and the length of the trip. Be sure to include some individually wrapped snacks for when the "hungries" attack and travel time is too precious to stop.

Today many families travel by plane. Some youngsters even travel alone under the watchful eye of a flight attendant. If they are flying to their destination, have your grandchildren compare the time it takes to fly with the time it would take to drive. Talk about the factors involved such as the rate of speed (approximate) that a car and plane might travel. Discuss and estimate the difference in miles between the routes of the plane and the car. You don't have to have actual mileage; you're just trying to help them see the vast difference between the methods of travel. Point out that when traveling by plane, they may encounter airport layovers, while rest stops are required when traveling by car.

Even if your grandchildren are flying, they will still appreciate a travel package. The older grandchildren will enjoy headsets, along with a music tape. Books will be welcomed by all ages. Consider a stuffed animal backpack for your younger grandchildren, the reason being twofold: They will have a place to keep their books, plus they will have the security of carrying a stuffed animal with them on the trip.

Your grandchildren may already have luggage, but if they don't, there are all kinds of cute bags and suitcases on the market. Some state, "I'm going to Grandma's." I've even seen some carry-on models with wheels and a pull handle. They're perfect for carrying those personal possessions through the airport. Shop for backpacks and bags for the older grandchildren too. They're growing up, but they're never too old for surprises.

In the days of the TV family the Waltons, three generations sometimes lived together. Today families live miles apart. Still, we are fortunate. Technology allows us to share family concerns quickly in spite of the difference in miles. Some families may get to visit quarterly, a couple times a year, or once a year. Other families may get to visit only every few years. Visits with extended family are exciting. Everyone gets butterflies as the long-awaited trip approaches. Then it arrives and zip, it's gone. But while you are together, let go of the cares and pressures of the day. Enjoy God's blessings as he brings you and your extended family together for a visit.

Family Vacations

Day trips are great for families who live only a few hours apart. Visit a zoo, museum, or historical sight. Each state has many sightseeing opportunities to offer. Present each of your grandchildren with a one-time-use camera. Children love to take their own pictures. This will provide them with personal mementos.

Families who live several states apart might consider meeting halfway. If there is a point of interest nearby, take a tour. Staying at a hotel and relaxing around the pool provide many hours of family togetherness.

Your extended family, whether separated by a long distance or just a few miles, might want to consider this next idea. Encourage your extended family to spend one week of the year together. I know several families who do this and it has blessed their lives. Busy lifestyles keep these families as separated as the miles. They have found that vacationing together is the answer to keeping family ties strong. They choose to go to a mountain or lake resort and get reacquainted. Family units are free to pursue their individual interests, but at some designated time of day, the entire extended family gets together for an activity. These types of get-togethers are restful for Grandma too. She gets to relax and enjoy the entire family. She is free from worrying about what to cook for the next meal or if she is keeping up with the laundry.

A Visit to Grandpa and Grandma's House

Vacations are great! Visiting family is great! But among my fondest childhood memories are the weeks spent at Grandpa and Grandma's house. I am a firm believer that, if possible, grandchildren should spend some days and nights with grandparents. Spending time together is how we really get to know each other. Time spent together reveals our likes and dislikes; it allows revelation of our personalities.

Grandparents, don't take on more than you can handle. Consider your health and the fact that you may not be used to a lively brood. Adjust the length of stay and the number of grandchildren involved so that it can be an enjoyable experience for you too. Then plan ahead for the visit. Cooking and freezing meals in advance will enable you to have more time to play with your grandchildren.

Grandparents seem younger all the time, so if you're up to a full house, invite all your grandchildren for a stay. Let cousins get acquainted with cousins; it may be the only time they will spend together. If you are experiencing a panic attack at the mere thought of having all your grandchildren together, have one or two of them visit at a time. This will allow even the shyest grandchild to be the center of attention.

I love the plaque that reads, "Grandmas are just antique little girls." Recently (I guess they didn't want to leave Grandpa out) I saw one that said, "Grandpas are just antique little boys." Both of these statements are true. In this childlike spirit, begin to plan your week. Your grandparents lived in a time that was slower in pace. Imagination was the creative force behind all play. Sometimes in this modern age, imaginations are allowed to lie dormant. Fill the time you spend with your grandchildren with imaginative, simple activities.

You and your grandchildren can go fishing, take a walk, throw pebbles in a stream and watch the ripples, collect rocks along a creek bank, work in the garden, pot some flowers, roast hotdogs, feed the animals (if you're fortunate enough to live on a farm), pick berries, make jam, cook a meal, make homemade ice cream, bake a pie, bake bread, lie under a shade tree and look at the sky through the leaves, watch the clouds drift by, catch lightning bugs, dig up fishing worms, walk to the post office, visit the library, have a picnic, or worship together. I realize that most of these activities are appropriate for rural areas. If you live in a city, take your grandchildren to a park or a museum. Your options are as limitless as your imagination.

My friend Carol Layman wrote an adaptation of a fairy tale for her grandchildren. During their visit, they devised costumes and practiced their parts. Then she videotaped the final production. What a memory they will have. Years from now they'll be saying, "Remember the year we went to Grandma's and did the play *Little Red Riding Hood*?"

Today garage sales are a sign of the times. But after you've cleaned your closets, put some of the items back for your grandchildren's visit. Stuff some discarded clothing, shoes, and jewelry into a suitcase. The children will delight in playing dress-up at Grandma's. Another friend Jean Glick allows her grandchildren to play with an old tea set. They can have a tea party any time of day. When you clean your kitchen cabinets, keep those odds and ends of dishes and let your grandchildren use them in their make-believe restaurant.

By now you get the idea. Weave into the fabric of your time together the simple things that can be shared— things that make memories and touch the heart.

Many children attend summer camp, so get creative and plan your own. Make up a name for your week of activities and your location. How about Grandpa and Grandma's Roundup, or shorten it to G & G Roundup, located in the rolling hills of Grandpa and Grandma's farm. Or Camp GC (grandchildren) located in the heartland of _____ (name your town and state). These are just a couple suggestions. You'll probably come up with a special name that will have significance for you and your grandchildren. A few weeks before the visit, send a special invitation to your grandchildren. Invitations may take the form of a letter, a computer made card, or a purchased invitation.

When I attended camp, we had a craft time each day. Designing T-shirts is a fun craft to commemorate the year and the name of your camp. Before your grand-children arrive, buy some plain white T-shirts to fit your grandchildren. Machine wash and dry them ahead of time. Choose glitzy markers and vibrant colors of paint from your craft store. In the same area of the store, look for a variety of sponge shapes. They can be used for dipping in paint and making designs on fabric. Aluminum pie pans are good to have on hand for this project. You can pour a small amount of paint in a pan, then let the children dip their sponge in the paint and apply it to their shirt. You'll probably want to let them practice on an old shirt first. That way they can get the feel for how hard to press. Have some water nearby to rinse out the sponges between colors. One year our grand-children painted pictures on their shirts representing the different activities of the week. Another year we used sponges cut in the shape of popsicles.

Looking for something different? Decorate hats with paints, jewels, sequins, and bits of ribbon. One thing you can be sure of—the kids will love their keepsakes. After they're home, your grandchildren will remember their special week at Grandpa and Grandma's each time they wear their creations.

Camp wouldn't be the same without watermelon, s'mores, and roasted hotdogs. While the wiener roast is in progress, roast some marshmallows for s'mores. Sandwich half a chocolate bar and two roasted marsh-mallows between two graham crackers. Yum, yum! Along about dusk, slice the watermelon and send the kids outside to eat it. Don't forget to have a seed spit-ting contest. Give everyone a wet paper towel to wipe their hands and mouths, then send them one by one to the shower. After the showers, get out the guitar or gather around the piano and sing some camp songs.

There are things to do and places to go in this modern day. Life was simple when we were kids and visited our grandparents. Enjoy the simple things of the heart with your grandchildren, but be sure to include some of the pleasurable outings available today. Take your grandchildren to a cinema or shopping mall. I love to take my grandchildren shopping. This is the only time I have an excuse to buy the adorable toys and clothes I admire all year. I *really* am a little girl at heart! Besides, I delight in giving presents.

By now I hope your mind is racing with plans for a summer camp with your grandchildren. As they drive off and you wave a tired, tearful farewell, the memories will be worth every aching bone in your body. But perk up! Rest up! And begin to plan for next year.

Family Reunions

Family reunions abound in the summer. If your children and grandchildren can't attend, don't let them miss out on their family heritage. Make a photo album or videotape of the event. If you decide on the album, include a newsy letter introducing each branch of the family.

What? Your family is spread across the country? If a family reunion is out of the question, host one by mail. Have each branch of the family put together a page of photographs and a newsletter. Head up the project and have them mail their pages to you. Photocopy the pages, put them in inexpensive folders, and mail the folders to your relatives. Presto! A reunion by mail. This could be better than the real thing!

Fourth of July

Scents from outdoor grills travel the breeze, intermingling throughout the neighborhood. Families gather to celebrate the Fourth of July. But hamburgers aren't the only things that sizzle on this festive day. Night falls and sparklers are lit, spitting bits of light into the velvety darkness. Grandchildren snuggle on grandparents' laps to watch the night sky explode with confetti-like sprays of fireworks. Add another candle. Sing another song. America is having another birthday!

Family vacations may enable your clan to be together over this bang-up holiday. If not, use some ingenuity and celebrate in heart, even if apart. Share cassette tape recordings about some Fourth of July celebrations you remember. In our small town we've had some memorable parades. If your grandchildren are in a parade and you can't attend, have your children videotape it or snap some pictures. Call each other up to say hello, and share the day's activities.

Grandma, share this idea for a flag cake before the big celebration arrives. You might want to write it on a recipe card for your grandchildren's files.

Flag Cake

1 package of white cake mix (any brand)	walnuts, pecans, or gold-foil-wrapped candies
1 container of white frosting	red candies or candied cherries
blue food coloring	

Bake a white cake in an oblong pan and ice the cake with white frosting. Tint a small amount of frosting with blue food coloring and ice one small area in the upper left corner with the blue frosting. Place thirteen walnuts, pecans, or gold-foil-wrapped candies in a circle on the blue frosting to represent the original thirteen colonies. Use red candies or candied cherries (cut in half) to form the red stripes on the cake.

If you like fruit, try using blueberries for the blue part of the flag and strawberries for the stripes. Be creative and use whatever your taste buds desire.

When I was a kid, getting together on the Fourth of July was an excuse to make homemade ice cream. What a treat! In this age of busyness, ice cream freezers seldom get used. Many families don't even have them. But what is a flag cake without ice cream? Mail this simple recipe to your grandchildren and let them try their hand at shaking up this ice cream delight.

Ice Cream Delight

2 plastic gallon-size bags with zip closures	3/4 cup of milk
	1 1/2 tbsp sugar
ice	1 tsp vanilla
6 tbsp table salt	

Fill one of the bags about half full with ice. Add six tablespoons of table salt. Fill the second bag with the milk, sugar, and vanilla. Place the second bag inside the bag of ice. Shake until solid. Enjoy!

In my day, when the extended family got together on the Fourth of July, we played together. Family gatherings were the one time that grown-ups joined the kids in outdoor games. Memories of playing croquet and badminton on sunny afternoons flood my mind. Horseshoe pitching and baseball were favorites among the men and boys. If you can't get together with your family, tell your grandchildren about the games you played as a child. Dig out the old croquet set from the attic or basement. Then the next time your grandchildren visit you, give them the family heirloom game. Just think, these kinds of gifts work for you in two ways: You share a memory and, at the same time, you're getting one more item cleaned out of your storage area.

If your heirloom game is in bits and pieces, consider giving your grandchildren a gift certificate. Gift certificates can be mailed, and because you suggest what the certificate is for (e.g., This is for an outdoor game), you've given thought to the gift. Yet, your grandchildren get to make the selection, choosing the color and style. If you are unable to get out and about, a friend can easily purchase a certificate for you to give.

Story Time

Hopefully this summer you will be able to personally read books to your little ones and watch videos together. But whether on tape or in person, continue your book sharing. Look for Mae Freeman's *Stars and Stripes* (Random House), *Grandaddy's Stars* by Helen Griffith, illustrated by James Stevenson (Green Willow Books), and *I Unpacked My Grandmother's Trunk* by Susan Hoguet (E. P. Dutton). The last one can be used as a travel game too. Choose books and videos with an outdoor theme or those filled with summer activities. Don't ignore the classics such as Johanna Spyri's *Heidi* and *Where the Red Fern Grows* by Wilson Rawls. Videos, as well as the books, are available. Spend an afternoon browsing in a bookstore, and you'll be brimming with all kinds of ideas. Books spark ideas for clever grand-parents to expand upon.

Perhaps visits with your extended family are out of the question. Maybe there won't be any family get-togethers. If this is your situation and you're feeling discouraged, my heart goes out to you.

When I was little, I marveled at my grandma. She had two sons and one daughter who lived overseas for several years. They each had children—her precious grandchildren. Their main contact was by mail. Once in a while there was a phone call. I was a tenderhearted child who sensed that Grandma's heart ached for them. Yes, her other children and grandchildren lived near her, but each person holds a special place within a family. I'm sure she wanted to be surrounded by all her children and grandchildren.

I have come to the conclusion that my grandma's faith in God was what enabled her to endure the sep-arations. She trusted God to care for her own. Today ask God to watch over your family wherever they may live. Be comforted by the knowledge that God is omnipresent. Hold that thought. Meditate upon it. Let it seep deep within your mind.

Even if you're miles apart, remember, your family can be near in heart!

Journaling Pages

My back was giving me fits. I had lain down on the couch to watch a movie with my grandchildren. Getting up was a struggle. As our ten-year-old grandson observed my agony, he said, "Grandma, as hard as it is for you to get up, I don't think you should lie down."

Wait 'til you hear what my grandchild said . . .

Here's a bright idea for long-distance grandparenting . . .

Name of grandchild

Long-distance activity

Date completed

Name of grandchild

Long-distance activity

Date completed

Name of grandchild

Long-distance activity

Date completed

Name of grandchild

Long-distance activity

Date completed

August

"Y ou've been kissed by angels!" my grandma would say whenever people teased me about the freckles on my nose. The summer sun always produced these gems due to my fair complexion. But Grandma made me feel good about myself. Grandparents have a way of doing that.

Swinging through Summer

August days are generally hot and lazy. Everyone has worked and played hard. In August, it is time to relax and enjoy the remaining days of summer. If you're sitting on a porch swing thinking about your grandchildren who live far away, write them a letter. Tell them about the swing you enjoyed as a child. Was it a rope swing with a board seat, a tire swing, or did you have a swing set?

Do your grandchildren have a swing set? Do they need new swings for an old swing set? Can you help with this project? Can you put up a swing or build a swing set during your next visit? Is there a tree in your grandchild's yard that would be sturdy enough for a rope swing?

If you don't have a porch swing that your grandchildren can enjoy when they come to visit, is there a park nearby with swings? There are few things as precious as a toddler's giggle when their tummy is tickled by the experience of swinging. Take some time for this simple but memorable experience.

Summer Fairs

County and state fairs are as American as apple pie. During the summer months they polka dot rural America. My earliest childhood memory of the fair is of riding the carousel. I didn't want the thrill of riding the horses up, down, and around to ever end. The music from the calliope heightened the adventure.

I would like to take my grandchildren to a fair, but unless the date falls during a visit, it is impossible. Perhaps you are a grandparent who has the same longing. You may see other people at the fair with their grandchildren and feel a twinge of envy. Your grandchildren are missing out on a memorable event that could be shared with you.

Good news! You don't have to feel bad. There are alternatives. During a recent visit with my extended family, I went shopping with my grandchildren. We were in a mall when, low and behold, we came upon a huge carousel. I was delighted and so were they. Naturally, we had a ride. What fun! Even though the setting was different, we shared an experience similar to a county fair. In the food court we even found foods similar to the concessions sold at a fair. Our favorites were the lemonade and hot pretzels. I know that many malls feature carousels, as do some children's museums. Today there are giant amusement parks all across our nation with midway atmospheres reminiscent of a fair.

If a visit is out of the question, consider sending money for tickets for a fair or amusement park in your extended family's area. Mail a single-use camera for them to photograph the day's events, or if they have a video camera, ask them to record the entire day for you. You can also take pictures of your county fair and mail them to your grandchildren. Maybe you can even get a picture of Grandpa on the Ferris wheel.

Birthdays

Birthdays occur in all months, but since our family happens to celebrate many of them in August, I've decided to address the subject here. I was devastated when I realized I would not be able to see my grandchildren on their birthdays. Just for the record, I'm not very good at celebrating events that aren't really on *the* day, but I've tried to grow up and accept the fact that many things are going to get in the way. Most celebrations have to be scheduled earlier or later than the actual date.

If your family is able to get together during the summer, take advantage of the opportunity and celebrate all the summer birthdays. When birthdays fall at times when you can't get together—and they will—use the telephone (you'll want to hear the excitement in your grandchildren's voices). Follow up by sending a videotape. The fax machine is great for sending homemade greeting cards complete with photos. Messages can also be sent by mail or e-mail.

Children love getting packages in the mail. Mail-order companies save grandparents the trouble of finding the right size box and getting together packaging materials. You might consider letting your grandchildren shop through a mail-order catalog and mark some items they would like to have. You can surprise them on their birthday with one of the items. This works well for Christmas too.

Magazine subscriptions are birthday gifts that keep giving all year. Be sure to check out the magazine by reading a few sample copies at the library. Know what you are giving.

Money in a card never fails to produce smiles. Some grandparents have a set amount that they mail to each grandchild, others mail a dollar for each year of a child's age. Either way, it is a welcome gift. Gift certificates are also appreciated. They allow teenagers to shop for what they want and save grandparents the hassle of sending items.

Grandchildren appreciate gifts that show you recognize they are growing up. An alarm clock is such a gift. Grandchildren welcome this grown-up gift. Birthdays are ideal times to start or add to collections. Music boxes, thimbles, tea sets, model cars, sports memorabilia, stamps, and coins are a few items that grandchildren might enjoy collecting.

A lady whom I met at a writers' conference told me she writes a story for her grandchildren on their birthdays. I marveled as she told me that she does this every year. They will have a grand collection by the time they reach adulthood. What a wonderful idea! The only cost is your time. Are you a songwriter? Write a song for your grandchild's birthday. Are you an artist?

Paint a picture. If these gifts seem overwhelming, try writing a birthday letter. The idea is to give a part of yourself. I have a journal that I am filling with all the cute things my grandchildren say. When they are grown, I intend to give each of them a copy. The collection will be a keepsake to treasure.

When birthdays arrive and you can't be there, try these ideas:

Send money and ask your child to order a balloon bouquet from Grandpa and Grandma to arrive on your grandchild's birthday.

Mail a single-use camera and have your child snap photos of your grandchild's birthday party. You can also send a videotape if the family has a camcorder.

Send your grandchildren a videotape with a birthday message from you. Share a memory of when you were his or her age.

Mail birthday napkins, plates, cups, balloons, and birthday hats in a design that will delight your grandchild.

Wrap small, inexpensive items—one for each year of your grandchild's life—and place them in a gift bag. Suggested items include personalized pens and pads, hair barrettes, bows, shoelaces, gum, candies, small cars, coin purses, and party favors.

Save newspaper headlines or magazines on your grandchild's birthday. Give them to your grandchild when he or she reaches adulthood.

Hand down family keepsakes appropriate for the age of your grandchild.

Experience has taught us which things will be valued in future years. Choose wisely the things to give your grandchildren. Whatever you do, birthdays are grand, even if you have to celebrate clear across the land!

Books and Videos

Instruct your grandchildren on how to build a tent over the clothesline using old sheets and blankets. Yes, I know there are all kinds of pup tents available, but I don't want them to miss out on the fun of creating their own tent. If there isn't a clothesline available, use a card table. Toss a blanket over it and presto! A tent!

August afternoons are perfect for hiding out in a tent nestled under a shade tree and listening to a tape of Grandma reading some good storybooks. The Franklin books written by Paulette Bourgeois and illustrated by Brenda Clark (Scholastic) are excellent. The books deal with common childhood problems. Some of the books about the young turtle-hero are *Franklin Is Bossy, Hurry Up Franklin, Franklin Fibs, Franklin Plays the Game, Franklin in the Dark, Franklin Is Messy, Franklin Wants a Pet,* and *Franklin Is Lost.* Combine the books with a toy turtle, and a smiling grandchild is guaranteed.

Mary Ann Hoberman is the author of *A House Is a House for Me,* which is illustrated by Betty Fraser and published by Puffin Books. *A House Is a House for Me* lists the homes for many different animals and objects. The book is ideal for children who have to move often. It helps them adjust to the idea that anywhere can be home.

Don't forget to send books for the older grandchildren to enjoy. Shop garage sales, library book sales, and used book stores for bargains. Look for classics and start your grandchildren on the road to literature appreciation.

Videos are a fun way to relax after a hard day of play. Bath time is over, pajamas are on—it's time to snuggle in for a good movie. Check out the videos in your local Christian bookstores. There are some great movies available that teach values. You may not be able to attend church with your little ones, but your life can be a witness. Many adults tell me that their grandparents made a difference in their lives through their Christian influence.

Also, don't miss the wonder of the classics. L. M. Montgomery's *Anne of Green Gables* is the perfect movie to lift your spirits. The scenery is beautiful, and the story is captivating. You won't want to watch this movie in one sitting. Instead, stretch it out, watching a little bit each night. I recommend that children read a section of the book, watch the corresponding part of the movie, then discuss the differences. You can follow this same procedure with William Armstrong's *Sounder.*

Remember, kids today have short attention spans. Sandwiching books with movies keeps all ages happy. When you purchase movies to mail to your grandchildren, check out copies of the same video from the library for you to watch. This will enable you to discuss the movie in a phone conversation or letter. Keep up with current movies and books too. Provide classics, but keep an eye open for new material. We've had wonderful writers in the past, and we have many talented writers today.

"Keep Cool" Care Package

August is the month when temperatures soar in most parts of the country. Send a "keep cool" care package to your grandchildren. Buy some popsicle molds and mail them along with some powdered drink mixes. The kids will love freezing their own pops. If you can't find the molds, purchase small plastic cups instead. A bag of popsicle sticks can be purchased at craft stores.

When it is too hot to be outside, remind your grandchildren to bring out Monopoly, Scrabble, and other board games. There are also many challenging computer games on the market. Kids like to be busy all the time so, Grandpa and Grandma, help Mom out by thinking of things for them to do.

If you are fortunate enough to have e-mail or a fax machine, begin a story and take turns adding to it. Remember, games can also be played via e-mail or fax.

All good things must come to an end, and that means summer vacation. Most schools are in session by mid-August. This month is a good time to send a back-to-school gift certificate. Your grandchildren will delight in picking out a lunch box, a special school supply, or even a new outfit. The gift will help soften the pangs of summer's end.

Blending the past with the present builds bridges to the future.

Journaling Pages

Our two-year-old grandson wanted to come home on the plane with me.

"But I have to teach school," I explained.

With sincerity, he announced, "I know how to pay tention."

Wait 'til you hear what my grandchild said . . .

_____

_____

_____

_____

_____

_____

_____

_____

Here's a bright idea for long-distance grandparenting . . .

_____

_____

_____

_____

_____

_____

_____

_____

_____

_____

Name of grandchild

Long-distance activity

Date completed

Name of grandchild

Long-distance activity

Date completed

Name of grandchild

Long-distance activity

Date completed

Name of grandchild

Long-distance activity

Date completed

September

risk mornings and cool evenings signal seasonal changes. When you have lived many years, changing seasons are easy to spot. Your grandchildren, however, with their busy schedules, often miss nature's signals. This is where Grandpa and Grandma's expertise is needed. Point out the signs in nature that alert us to seasonal changes. Videotape a nature walk, make a cassette tape, or write a letter. Let your eyes be their eyes. Mail your grandchildren a list of things to look for, and send them on a scavenger hunt. Share some stories about the Septembers you experienced as a child.

Fun with Leaves

Autumn means falling leaves. Before the leaves get too dry, suggest that your grandchildren make leaf rubbings. If you are making a videotape of your nature walk, add this demonstration to your tape.

Gather different kinds of leaves. Place a leaf face down and place a plain sheet of paper over it. Using a crayon, rub across the paper to make an imprint. Using different kinds of leaves and different colors of crayon will create eye-catching autumn foliage. Add a final touch by painting a blue watercolor wash over the entire picture or coloring the picture lightly with a blue crayon. These pictures make lovely gifts when placed in an inexpensive frame.

My daughter and grandchildren made beautiful fall sweatshirts using leaves for all the grandparents. They dipped leaves in a small amount of paint and pressed them onto the front and sleeves of a cream colored sweatshirt. Claiming the promise "Never will I leave you; never will I forsake you" (Heb. 13:5), they added, "God Never Leaves Me." The results were "cool" sweatshirts to wear in the brisk autumn air.

Early September is a good time to gather leaves for a leaf book. The leaves are full sized, and it is possible to find them before they become too dry. This is an activity for both grandparents and grandchildren. If you live in different areas of the country, you can have double the fun and double the learning. Gather every kind of leaf you can find in your geographical region. Be sure to identify the leaf and the area of the country in which it was found. Corresponding about this family project will add depth to your relationships.

As you gather the leaves, place individual leaves between wax paper and then press them between books. When the leaves are pressed, place them on paper and laminate the pages with clear contact paper. You may then place the pages in a three-ring binder. Or if you prefer, preserve your leaves in a photo album containing pages with clear plastic coverings. Grandparents, if your state laws permit, mail your leaf findings to your grandchildren. Have them add your leaf pages to their book.

Autumn Activities

Toward the end of September, the leaves will have started to fall. Here's your chance to share some stories of autumn. By the way, most grandchildren won't be familiar with the word *autumn.* Everyone refers to this season as fall. But *autumn* is such a beautiful word, I think we should at least make sure our grandchildren are introduced to it. Who knows, it may catch on again. Tell your grandchildren about the leaf forts you built as a child. Maybe you can even encourage them to rake the leaves where they live. Mom and Dad probably won't mind if they play in the leaves for a while before bagging them. I love the smell of burning leaves, but discuss why we bag them today.

It's time to snap that seasonal postcard photo of your home. If your grandchildren live in a tropical climate where there are few autumn leaves, they'll be even more delighted to see the foliage in your area. The autumn stories will be especially meaningful to them because it will be different than what they are accustomed to. Maybe Mom and Dad will want to plan a trip to visit at this colorful time of the year. Depending on how far apart you live, you may want to meet halfway in a state that has fall foliage. The climate will affect when the fall foliage peaks, so you may want to plan the trip for October.

The Fall of Freddie the Leaf by Leo Buscaglia, Ph.D. (Slack), is a story about the cycle of life. This seasonal book is helpful in explaining the seasons of life. Challenge your grandchildren to visit the library, look in their science books at school, or find information on their computers about why leaves change color. When fall officially arrives on September 23, have them do a little research and find out where the sun is located at this time. How does the sun's position affect the length of days and nights? Fax your research back and forth or write it in a letter. Now is the time to look for signs of animal migration and hibernation. You may also want to discuss what the farmers are doing in the field.

Don't always give your grandchildren the answers, but don't let them get frustrated searching alone either. Instead, team up with them and get your children involved. Chances are, everyone will remember the information if they help discover the answers. These experiences will help you bond with your grandchildren and strengthen your ties with your adult children.

Labor Day

We celebrate Labor Day on the first Monday of September. Families often view this holiday as the last hurrah of summer. Most choose to spend the three day weekend participating in outdoor activities.

Many children do not realize that Labor Day is a day set aside to honor working people. Introduce your grandchildren to what God says about work and rest. Share Exodus 20:9–10 with your grandchildren: "Six days you shall labor and do all your work, but the seventh day is a Sabbath to the LORD your God. On it you shall not do any work, neither you, nor your son or daughter, nor your manservant or maidservant, nor your animals, nor the alien within your gates."

Here is your opportunity to discuss God's Word with your grandchildren. Point out the wisdom of resting from work. Our stress-filled days place many demands on us. We would all benefit from applying this godly principle to our lives. Discuss ways that your family can honor the Sabbath. Speculate as to how observing the Sabbath would improve emotional and physical health.

National Grandparents Day

In 1979, President Jimmy Carter proclaimed the first Sunday following Labor Day as National Grandparents Day. Many schools recognize grandparents by inviting them to visit their grandchildren's classrooms. The students often present a program. If your grandchild extends a special invitation, by all means attend. When schedules and miles keep you apart on these special days, write a letter or make a cassette tape telling about an event from your school days. Send a picture of Grandpa and Grandma for each grandchild.

As an elementary teacher, I have my students write interview questions and mail them to their grandparents. The grandparents who get to attend the special day may share their stories in class. Students who receive taped interviews may share them as they receive them. This way no grandparent or grandchild is left out. If you receive interview questions from one of your grandchildren, take the time to answer indepth. One of the most priceless things I have is an interview that my daughter had with her paternal grandfather. He told of living through the depression.

If your grandchild has trouble thinking of questions, here are some things you may want to share about your school days:

How did you get to school? If you rode a bus, how long was your bus ride?

Did you take your lunch? If so, what kind of foods did you pack?

How big was your school? Was it a rural or a city school?

What was your teacher like?

What kind of desks did you have?

Share your favorite school story.

What kind of grades did you make?

Did you ever get into trouble? Do you dare tell about it?

What type of clothes were in style?

Tell about your friends.

By now your memory video is probably on rewind, viewing scenes from yesteryear. Share everything you can remember. Invite your grandchildren to share about their school days too. Allow your grandchildren to honor you by cooperating fully. In the days and months ahead, you may want to reciprocate by writing each grandchild a letter sharing how much he or she means to you.

Autumn Means Apples

Chances are your grandchildren have learned about John Chapman, better known as Johnny Appleseed, but only grandmas can tell their grandchildren which apples make the best pies, applesauce, and so on.

Are you a grandmother who can peel an entire apple without breaking the peeling? Demonstrate this on a videotape, and share how you learned to do it. Do you have an apple peeler with a handle that you turn to peel an apple in seconds? Show the grandchildren how it works. If you no longer use it, mail it to them. They'll be delighted to use this device. Don't be surprised when they peel all the apples in their refrigerator. An apple slicer that slips down over an apple and removes the core is inexpensive and can be easily mailed. Older children or moms can easily maneuver this tool.

Make a videotape of you stirring up some appealing apple recipes: apple pies, apple dumplings, apple turnovers, applesauce, apple cake, apple butter, fried apples, stewed apples, baked apples (try baking them in the microwave), apple crisp, apple pancakes, and many others. Whether you are baking from scratch or creating instant dishes with ready-made ingredients, your grandchildren will love seeing and hearing Grandma demonstrate her specialties.

The supermarket where I shop has an apple recognition chart. These charts can also be found in recipe books and at the library. The chart shows a picture of an apple, names the apple, describes the flavor, and suggests the apple dishes that that particular apple is best suited for. Buy one of several different kinds of apples and present this information on your videotape or write the information on recipe cards to be filed away.

Read your Johnny Appleseed stories and other apple books to your grandchildren either on videotape or on cassette tape. An excellent book, *Apples,* is by Ann L. Burckhardt (Bridgestone Books). This easy reader has bright, colorful photographs of apples. The book discusses different kinds of apples, the parts of an apple, where and how apples grow, and it even touches on the history of this delectable fruit. Another fun book is Jennifer Storey Gillis's *An Apple a Day* (Storey Communications). This wonderful book is ideal for parents and grandparents, for it is filled with projects and recipes for children. Puzzles, history, and games are also included.

While you're videotaping, include an apple craft for the older grandchildren. You might want to slice apples and dry them in the oven. Create apple wreaths and garlands, accenting with cinnamon sticks and country ribbon. These decorative crafts fill your home with the delightful smell of a freshly baked pie.

Cut an apple diagonally and let your grandchildren discover the surprise star that hides within. Take out the seeds and plant them in a Styrofoam cup. Talk about the life cycle of the apple: seed, plant, tree, blossom, and fruit. Discuss the seasons in relationship to the apple cycle.

Did you have apple trees on your property as a child? Do you have apple trees now? Do they? Share the best thing about having fruit trees. Then share the most unpleasant part, such as picking up fruit before you can mow the lawn. Encourage your children to take your grandchildren to an orchard. Keep the mail and communication wires hot as you share information back and forth.

May you and the apples of your eye enjoy many appealing apple activities!

Journaling Pages

Our son-in-law traveled a lot and would often talk to our two-year-old grandson on the phone. One weekend, the toddler made some reference to "this dad said" and "that dad said."

When his parents questioned him, he explained that he had a dad on the phone and a dad at home. Our son-in-law tried to clear it up by calling his young son on their portable phone. As he visibly stood talking to his son over the portable phone, the toddler held the other phone tightly to his ear.

"Look, son, here I am!"

Excitedly, the toddler quipped, "I have 'this dad' and 'that dad'!"

"No, son, you have one dad. My voice is just going through the phone."

Puzzled, our grandson asked, "How does it do that?"

Wait 'til you hear what my grandchild said . . .

Here's a bright idea for long-distance grandparenting . . .

Name of grandchild

Long-distance activity

Date completed

Name of grandchild

Long-distance activity

Date completed

Name of grandchild

Long-distance activity

Date completed

Name of grandchild

Long-distance activity

Date completed

October

*J*ack Frost has completed his painting. Autumn is now gowned in her finest. Shades of crimson, butterscotch, and russet decorate the countryside. Roadside markets are well stocked with pumpkins, gourds, and potted chrysanthemums. Festivals and craft shows abound and provide economical entertainment for families. Enjoy the last few days of splendor before winter.

Columbus Day

The month begins with the celebration of Columbus Day. Students learn about this holiday in school, but Grandparents, you can help make the information stick by encouraging your grandchildren to relay the facts to you or by expanding the study. Sometimes teachers don't have the time to go as in-depth as they'd like. Be sure to call or write and discuss the important facts and events surrounding Columbus Day.

Columbus Day is the perfect time to present your grandchildren with a globe. There are so many neat ones on the market. Do your grandchildren have a CD-ROM? If so, perhaps a CD of a world atlas would be a welcomed gift. Share a book or video about Columbus

Day. You may purchase these items, or find them in your library and recommend them to your grandchildren.

Send a box of Berry Blue Jell-O, clear plastic punch cups, and miniature ships or boats. Instruct Mom or the older grandchildren to create the ocean snack by letting the Jell-O set in the clear plastic punch cups. Mom can add some Cool Whip for the ocean waves. Top with miniature ships or boats from a party shop.

Plenty of Pumpkins

By now the pumpkin seeds you sent to your grandchildren have produced a plentiful pumpkin patch. If not, persuade your children to take the kids to a pumpkin patch, and let each grandchild pick out a pumpkin, compliments of you. Meanwhile, make a videotape demonstrating the many activities that can be done using pumpkins.

Tell your grandchildren to measure around all the pumpkins using a measuring tape and to record the measurements. Ask them if they think the size of the pumpkin has anything to do with the number of seeds inside. Next they should cut off the top of each pumpkin and scoop out the inside. After counting the seeds in each pumpkin, have them wash the seeds, pat them dry, and place them on a sprayed cookie sheet. Tell them to sprinkle the seeds with salt and bake them at 325 degrees for twenty to thirty minutes until crispy. Grandchildren will enjoy this healthy snack. You will too!

While you are in the process of making your tape, share how to make a pumpkin pie from scratch. Today there are many ways to cook a pumpkin. Wash the pumpkin, then cut off the top and remove the seeds and pulp. Set the pumpkin (without the lid) in a pan of water in the oven and bake it until the sides of the pumpkin are tender. It takes approximately one hour at 325 degrees. You can use the same method using a microwave, but in a shorter amount of time. You can also cut up your pumpkin, add a little water, and cook it in a Crock-Pot. The pumpkin will be ready to use in a pie or other recipes when the family returns home in the evening. You can also cut up a pumpkin and boil it in water on top of the stove until the pumpkin is soft. After your pumpkin is cooked, mash it and run it through a strainer.

Get out your favorite recipe book and follow the recipe for a pumpkin pie. Many children think pumpkin comes only in a can. Challenge older children to make pies both from scratch and from canned pumpkin. Which do they think is the best? If there is a camcorder available, ask Mom or Dad to videotape the grandchildren's pie baking. If not, have the children write and tell you their findings.

Explore recipes for pumpkin breads, pumpkin rolls, and pumpkin cookies. Fill up the remainder of the videotape by reading some delightful pumpkin tales. *The Biggest Pumpkin Ever* by Steven Kroll (Holiday) is a delightful story about two mice feeding on the same pumpkin. Browsing through your library and bookstore will provide you with many other pumpkin tales to share with your grandchildren.

Halloween and Harvest Events

Whether it is a Halloween or a harvest party, your grandchildren will probably want to dress up in a costume. As a grandparent, you can steer them toward fun and creative costumes. Encourage them to dress up as storybook or biblical characters, candy (M & M's, a Hershey Kiss, a Tootsie Pop), cereal boxes, or appliances. Stir their imaginations, and come up with a creative design. If you plan early enough, Grandma may even be able to help with the sewing. When party time arrives, have Mom and Dad snap some photos of the grandchildren in their costumes. Remind them to check double prints when they drop off the film at the lab so the extended family can enjoy a set too.

Research where Halloween originated and how it came to be celebrated in America. Have the older grandchildren participate in the research either at the library or on the computer. Compile the information, faxing or mailing it back and forth. Discuss how the holiday was celebrated in your youth. On the negative side, point out the direction that the celebration seems to be taking in this modern age. Trick-or-treating used to be a safe activity for youngsters. Now, children can trick-or-treat only at homes where they know the people, and they must be accompanied by an adult. Halloween pranks used to be harmless, now there are many harmful things done on this night.

On the other hand, many churches and communities are getting involved and trying to steer the holiday in a more positive direction. They are having harvest parties and getting the community involved in providing a safe Halloween for the neighborhood youngsters.

Share what the Bible teaches about the occult (Deut. 18:9–14). The world treats psychic readings, séances, Ouija boards, and horoscopes as if they were innocent, fun-loving, and amusing activities. Many Halloween parties may feature a séance as the evening's entertainment, especially at parties for pre-teens and teens. Children of this age are intrigued with the spine chilling, the gory, and the supernatural. They need to be warned about occult activities. If your grandchildren don't already know how to use a concordance, teach them how to use one. Train them to turn to the Scriptures to discover the answers to their questions.

Have your grandchildren consider their research, the current way Halloween is being celebrated in America, and the things they discover in the Scriptures. Based on this information, ask for their opinions about this holiday. Involve them in a letter writing discussion. Letter writing works better than telephoning, because it allows the participants time to think through their thoughts. Will a harvest party allow the fun activities to remain and focus on fellowship with friends? Is it possible for a family to decide to keep Halloween, ignoring those who want to turn it into something evil? Together, decide your family's stand regarding this holiday.

Spiders and Owls and Bats—Oh, My!

Whether you agree or not, spiders, owls, bats, and things that go bump in the night tend to occupy the interests of many youngsters during October. Instead of fighting these interests, why not guide them? *Stellaluna* by Janell Cannon (Scholastic) is a children's book about a baby bat who gets separated from her mother. Read the story on tape, and mail a copy of the book to your grandchildren. If books are too costly for your budget, check them out at the library and videotape yourself reading the books. The children can find the books at their library. After reading *Stellaluna,* challenge your older grandchildren to do some research on the different kinds of bats.

Children who experience insecurity when Mom leaves them in another's care will be encouraged by *Owl Babies.* The book is written by Martin Waddell and illustrated by Patrick Benson (Candlewick Press). Be sure to send black construction paper, stick pretzels to be used for branches, and some cotton balls so the grandchildren can create a picture of the baby owls. You may want to send a sample picture as an example for your grandchildren to follow. Lay the pretzels on the paper, forming tree branches. Glue down the pretzels and let them dry. Place two cotton balls, one above the other, on a pretzel branch and glue. The bottom cotton ball is for the body of the owl, and the top one is for the head. Cut eyes and a beak from black construction paper and place them on the top cotton ball. They'll love snacking on the extra pretzels as they pursue this artistic endeavor.

Spider books abound. It's always fun to snuggle up with a copy of *Charlotte's Web.* Follow this up with some research about spiders. If your grandchildren are studying spiders in school, have them write or fax you the information. Relaying the facts will help them remember the information. Small children will enjoy the song and book called *The Itsy, Bitsy Spider* by Iza Trapani (G. Stevens). Check your library and bookstore for more spider books.

Begin the month of October by starting a story web. Set some ground rules—no murders, blood, or gore—

just spooky. You may have to explain that spooky is when things seem to be frightening, but in the end, one discovers a logical explanation for the occurrence. If they still don't grasp what you're after, try this example: You're in bed, and you hear a tap, tap, tapping in the attic. The next day you investigate and discover a squirrel, mouse, or bird is responsible for the noise, or perhaps the wind is blowing through a crack in the attic.

Twist three black chenille sticks together at their centers, and spread them apart in a circular fashion. The six chenille arms will form the skeleton of the web. Tie a piece of black yarn (two yards long) at the center of the sticks, and secure it with a knot. Wrap the yarn loosely over and around each stick. Do not pull tightly or your circle will fold up. Each time you go around the circle, move the string outward an inch, then continue wrapping. Begin the tale, and mail the web and the story to the oldest grandchild. You will have to fold up the web each time you mail it. Draw the children a diagram of what the web looks like when it's open. They'll soon catch on to what you are trying to do. Have them add to the story and the web, passing them on to the next grandchild. If you have only one grandchild, mail the story and the web back and forth, with you winding up the tale. When the web is finished, knot the yarn around the last chenille stick and use the remaining yarn to hang up the web.

Bedtime Surprises

By now the nights are cool, and school is well in progress. Here are some suggestions for helping parents get their children to bed at a decent time:

Send a short bedtime video. State that the video may only be watched after everyone is ready for bed. Invite them to sip apple juice and eat pretzels as they view the bedtime movie selection. You can mail funds for these treats.

Plan a phone call to your grandchildren. Most homes have more than one phone, so you could have a conference call with two or three grandchildren in the same family. A phone call is a great way to unwind after a day's activities.

Mail a cassette tape to your grandchildren, and ask them to read from their school reader after they are ready for bed. If they do this on a regular basis throughout the year, you will be able to keep abreast of their progress, praising and encouraging them accordingly.

Mail new mugs for bedtime drinks. The drinks may be enjoyed while your grandchildren are listening to their sleepy time tapes.

With the seasonal change, new pajamas may be in order. New pajamas are practical and they always make bedtime a more welcome event. Practical gifts of sheets, blankets, and towel sets are available with character designs. The grandchildren will welcome these extra special touches and drift off to dreamland thinking about Grandpa and Grandma.

Begin and end your day by connecting with your grandchild through prayer and activity.

Journaling Pages

　　After our daughter's family moved several states away, I showed up unexpectedly and surprised our grandchildren at the airport. They were stunned. Our nine-year-old granddaughter finally regained her composure enough to explain why she had just stood there. "I thought that woman looked like my grandma, and she had my grandma's clothes on. But I knew it couldn't be. I didn't want to go up and kiss a stranger."

Wait 'til you hear what my grandchild said . . .

Here's a bright idea for long-distance grandparenting . . .

Name of grandchild

Long-distance activity

Date completed

Name of grandchild

Long-distance activity

Date completed

Name of grandchild

Long-distance activity

Date completed

Name of grandchild

Long-distance activity

Date completed

November

According to the calendar, it is still autumn. But in Indiana, late fall brings winter-like weather. Flax colored weeds line the roadsides, and cornstalks dot the fields. Trees with broomstick branches stretch upward, making silhouettes against the sky. Squirrels scamper to and fro, stockpiling food for winter.

Inside, a pot of soup simmers on the stove, steaming up the windows. The spicy aroma of baking pumpkin pie fills the house with a heavenly scent. Dusk falls early, and the room is lit with a soft lamp. Someone turns on the TV to listen to the evening news. November has arrived in Indiana.

Squirrel Watching

Do your grandchildren have a squirrel in their yard? Ask them. I'll bet they do. Correspond about the squirrel in your yard and the squirrel in their yard. Have them write a story about their squirrel and illustrate it. If they live in a tropical climate, take pictures and entertain them with stories of the squirrel in your yard. Older children can do some research on the many dif-

ferent types of squirrels. Check at the library and recommend some good storybooks for the little ones.
Encourage them to be aware of nature all around them.
Beatrix Potter watched animals as a child. Out of that
came her classics: *Squirrel Nutkin, Peter Rabbit,* and
many others. Who knows, you may be nurturing a bud-
ding author.

Thanksgiving

Thanksgiving will soon arrive, so think about celebrating this season of thankfulness all month long. Perhaps your extended family is going to be able to get
together for this holiday. That is a major thing to be
thankful for. If not, phone calls have a way of reaching
out and shortening the miles between loved ones, and
there are many ways to establish Thanksgiving traditions across the miles. Start a thanksgiving letter. Mail
it from family to family, asking each one to write about
the past year and the things they are thankful for. Plan
to read it on Thanksgiving Day or fax it if you can't be
together. Letters can be saved from year to year and
placed in a scrapbook. This tradition will provide a
wonderful legacy to be passed down through the generations. Grandparents can write or record on tape
Thanksgiving memories. They can also write an "I'm
thankful for you" letter to each grandchild. These
pages can also be added to the scrapbook.

Traditional Dishes

When you think about Thanksgiving, you probably
think about traditional dishes such as turkey, stuffing,

and all the trimmings. But each family has its own version of these foods. Whether together or apart, be sure to share your recipes, making copies for your grandchildren's recipe boxes. In our family, homemade noodles and sweet potato casserole rank high on our Thanksgiving menu. Grandma, take a minute and think about your Thanksgiving dishes. Share those recipes now. There's comfort in knowing that even though families may be separated by miles, they are sharing things in common.

The Pilgrims

One year our young grandson was fascinated with Native American artifacts. I made him a Native American costume. Our granddaughters wanted to dress in costume too. So with a little inventiveness, we came up with some pilgrim outfits. I thought this would be a onetime costume affair. But the next year, the little ones asked for the dress-up clothes. Thus, a tradition was born. The younger grandchildren enjoy dressing in authentic costumes reminiscent of the first Thanksgiving. Would your grandchildren like to do this? Even if you can't get together, you could mail the costumes.

Have your grandchildren pretend they are sailing on the Mayflower. Select a good storybook about the pilgrims' first voyage. If the grandchildren are coming to visit or if you're traveling to them, you can be in on the fun. If you can't be together, read the book to them on tape or video. Encourage them to act out the story. Being separated by distance will require that you enlist Dad, Mom, or older grandchildren to help with the sailing activity. Have them line up kitchen chairs or use the space between two twin beds for their ship. The point is to create a narrow space representing the cramped conditions on the ship. Have the grandchildren dress in costumes and settle on board.

The pilgrims could take only one trunk per family when they sailed. Suggest that each grandchild take a shoe box or small suitcase with one change of clothes, a Bible, and one toy. The pilgrims ate hardtack (cold biscuits) and salted meat for many of their meals. Mom can prepare a similar snack using biscuits and dried beef for the grandchildren to try. Have the children stay on their ship for at least thirty minutes—or a length of time that seems like a long time for the little ones. Have them imagine what it would be like to stay on the ship for many weeks. Acting out a story is a wonderful way to remember facts. It's a fun way to learn.

When you're making your reading tape, be sure to include *Samuel Eaton's Day* and *Sarah Morton's Day.* Both books were written by Kate Waters. The photos are by Russ Kendall (Scholastic). These are beautiful books. Even the adults and older grandchildren will enjoy them. They invite us to step back in time and refresh our memories of the past. These books lay the groundwork for more November activities.

Movie videos about the life of Squanto will help the children understand more about this period in history. Older grandchildren will enjoy reading more in-depth books about Squanto's life. Of course, if you watch a movie, you'll want some popcorn—especially with this story. In fact, celebrate Squanto's introduction of popcorn to the pilgrims with the following popcorn activities.

Popcorn

Mail some packs of different flavored popcorn to the grandchildren. Tell them that the pilgrims and early settlers ate popcorn like cereal. Encourage them to try it with milk and sugar. The brave and daring will be surprised to find out that it's good. String popcorn (send string and needles for this purpose) and place the garlands outside on tree branches for the birds. The children can also string popcorn and save the garlands for the Christmas tree, if Mom says it's okay.

Fix popcorn using several different methods. Many children think popcorn can be made only in the microwave or an air popper. Have Dad pour a little oil in a covered pan and pop some corn on the stove. Show them a picture of an old-fashioned popcorn popper. Today you can purchase popcorn that is still on the cob. Butter the corn and place the cob in the microwave bag that comes with it. Follow the directions for cooking time. This allows the grandchildren to see that popcorn does grow on a cob. This novelty can be purchased in a gourmet food section.

Books and Crafts

When you're sharing books, introduce the older grandchildren to the Foxfire books (Anchor Press/Doubleday). These lovely books will provide the children with many interesting facts about their American heritage and will help the younger generation appreciate the past.

Two other delightful books that can be read on tape are *Salt Hands* by Jane Chelsea Arragon, illustrated by Ted Rand (Penguin Books), and *The Cornhusk Doll* by Evelyn Minshull, illustrated by Edwin B. Wallace (Herald Press). Not only are the books well written but both have beautiful illustrations. You will want to accompany your tape with copies of the books if possible.

When you're visiting the library or bookstore, look for a craft book on making cornhusk dolls. This is an excellent activity to accompany the reading of *The Cornhusk Doll.* If you live where corn is raised, you may have access to cornhusks. Grandmas can demonstrate how to make a cornhusk doll on videotape or mail completed dolls to the grandchildren. Older grandchildren who are into crafts will be delighted if you mail the directions and supplies to them.

Spiritual Instruction

Grandparents, the celebration of Thanksgiving provides the perfect opportunity for you to introduce some spiritual teachings from the Bible. Early in the month, mail your grandchildren a cornucopia, nine pieces of plastic fruit, a roll of tape, and some paper tags. Write the children a letter reminding them that in order to have a harvest, the seed had to be planted, cultivated, and nourished. Then point them to Galatians 5:22–23. Discuss the fruit that can be harvested from a Spirit-controlled life. Encourage them to plant spiritual seed by inviting the Holy Spirit into their hearts and by being filled with the Spirit on a daily basis through prayer and Bible reading. To help them remember the fruit of the Spirit, have the grandchildren label the pieces of fruit and use them as decorations in their home. Fix a cornucopia for yourself too. This decoration can be saved from year to year.

Search the psalms, and challenge your grandchildren to do likewise, keeping a journal of thanksgiving Scriptures. Share your findings and watch your collection of thanksgiving Scriptures grow. You might want to send your grandchildren a clothbound journaling book to write their Scriptures in, or a small notebook will do. Research the Festival of Tabernacles, or Ingathering, celebrated by the Israelites as a thanksgiving for the harvest.

A thankful heart is a praying heart, so follow up by making a prayer box for each of your grandchildren. A prayer box can be a small cloth-covered box, a box crafted by needlepoint, a file box, or any small container. The box may be decorated however you choose. Be creative! Its purpose is to hold the praise listings or prayer requests of your grandchildren. Make sure they understand and respect the fact that a prayer box is private, like a diary.

The box I have is four inches square, fashioned from plastic needlepoint and yarn. A friend gave it to me, and I treasure it. A rose and a strand of pearls adorn the lid. Inside, I keep some small stones. When I pray, I visualize placing them before the cross. Sometimes the stones represent praise items. Other times they stand for a person I'm bringing before the Lord, or perhaps a problem that I leave with the Lord. Instruct your grandchildren to use their prayer boxes however God leads them.

Pretzels

End the season of thanksgiving with this tasty activity. It is believed that the first pretzels were made by German monks as a reward for children who learned to say their prayers. The pretzel shape represents the crossed arms of children at prayer. Share this bit of information with your grandchildren. Then have their parents purchase some frozen bread dough. Bread stick dough is excellent for this activity. Give a small portion of dough and a piece of waxed paper to each child. Have them form their dough into a long roll by rolling it on the wax paper. Then twist the dough into a pretzel shape, representing praying hands. Have Mom brush the pretzels with beaten egg white and sprinkle with salt. Bake them until they're golden brown (about ten minutes). If this activity is not possible, write or tape the story, then mail it with a container of twisted pretzels.

Remember, the family that prays together, stays together. Unite with thankful hearts!

Journaling Pages

Grandpa was preparing the Thanksgiving turkey for roasting. Our youngest grandson was watching. "Grandpa, where did you get that bird?"

"Oh, from the bird factory," Grandpa replied jokingly.

Later, our grandson was playing with some stuffed animals. He came running up to me with a toy bird and announced, "I've been hunting and I'm sending this bird to the bird factory."

Wait 'til you hear what my grandchild said . . .

_____

_____

_____

_____

_____

_____

Here's a bright idea for long-distance grandparenting . . .

_____

_____

_____

_____

_____

_____

_____

Name of grandchild
Long-distance activity

Date completed
Name of grandchild
Long-distance activity

Date completed
Name of grandchild
Long-distance activity

Date completed
Name of grandchild
Long-distance activity

Date completed

December

The harvest is over and the first snow has fallen. One step into the mall tells us that the Christmas season has arrived. Hopefully your children and grandchildren will be arriving for the holidays or you'll be going to their home. Impossible? Then what are you going to do? You have two choices: You can cry or you can hang in there, making the best of a difficult situation. I suggest you have a good cry, then choose the latter. But the question is how?

Christmas

Decorations

Hang in there by hanging your children's and grandchildren's pictures on the Christmas tree. Buy wallet-size picture frames to fit your decor, attach ribbon bows, and space the pictures about on your tree. Presto! You have the whole family home for Christmas. Keep in touch by phone and videos and you'll be close in heart, even if you are miles apart.

Be sure to snap some photos or videotape your decorations inside and outside your home. If you are videotaping, be sure to explain to your grandchildren where and how family traditions and decorations originated.

Ask your children to trace your grandchildren's handprints on multiple patterns of fabric. Cut out the handprints and decorate them with lace and ribbon at the wrist to make ornaments that add a special touch to Grandpa and Grandma's Christmas tree. Just seeing the handprints makes grandparents feel connected to their little ones.

Grandparents, choose some of your ornaments and send them to your sons and daughters. They can explain the significance of the ornaments to your grandchildren. In this manner, tradition is passed from one generation to the next. Christmas past becomes Christmas present. There is comfort in knowing that objects from each home are intermingled.

Miniature Boxes

Grandma, save your Christmas cards to form miniature boxes. To make a miniature box, cut the card on the fold. Fold all the sides up, one or two inches, depending on the size of the card. Cut one side of each corner on the fold so the sides overlap. Staple the corners to form a box. Do this with each piece of the card. The front of the card is used for the top of the box. The inside of the card is used for the inside bottom of the box.

Once your boxes are made, you can use them in place of an advent calendar or for surprises. Wrapped candies and Scripture verses may be placed inside the colorful creations. If you have several grandchildren in one family, send one set of twenty-five boxes. The grandchildren can take turns opening them, one for each day of December leading to Christmas. The child who opens the box gets to read the enclosed Scripture for the family's devotional time.

This inexpensive project can be done while watching TV. You'll have the boxes finished before you know it. Then pack the miniature boxes in a shoe box for easy mailing. What a smart grandma you are! You are helping your extended family focus on the Christmas story, and you're recycling too.

Christmas Memories

Whether you are writing a letter or making a cassette or videotape, tell the stories of Christmases past. Give your children and grandchildren a big dose of their Christmas heritage. What are the Christmas traditions that your family has handed down? Do you have stories from your grandparents? I can't emphasize this too many times: Tell the stories that won't be told unless you tell them.

I remember that Grandpa Colsher always managed to get angel hair on his black sweater. Grandma Black put cotton balls on her tree to look like snow. When I was a youth, silver foil icicles were frequently used. When I was really small, artificial trees didn't exist. The artificial silver trees with the multicolored spotlights were the rage when I was in high school, then came the artificial evergreens. When I was a child, strings of lights contained large bulbs. The miniature lights that are so prevalent today were still just a twinkle in someone's imagination. All of these innovations have provided us with better and safer ways to decorate for Christmas.

Have each adult in the family—grandparents, aunts, uncles, and cousins—share a Christmas memory. This

can be done when those who live in the same geographical region get together to share the holidays. This
makes a wonderful videotape gift. But if this isn't possible, take lots of pictures and get double prints. If the
extended family can't come home, send home to them.

Gift Giving

When you are a long-distance grandparent, you have
to shop early. Packages need to be mailed within the
first week or two of December. There is an advantage
to this. When your friends are in a last minute frenzy,
still shopping on the twenty-fourth, you will be finished
with your shopping. There are many ways to handle
your gift giving. Choose the method that is best suited
to your budget, circumstances, and family needs.

Let your grandchildren look through a catalog and
mark the items they might like. If both of you have the
same catalog, "I want" items may be marked during a
phone conversation. Your grandchildren can give you
the page numbers, guiding you to their selections.
Check with Mom before ordering so you don't dupli-
cate items. Then have the catalog company ship the
item directly to your grandchild. With this method you
don't have to fuss with the mailing.

A family keepsake makes an ideal gift. Do you have
something special you want to share with a particular
grandchild? You may want to consider giving it as a
Christmas gift.

Do you and your grandchildren share a similar interest? Christmas may be the perfect time to add to the
hobby. Have Grandpa build a dollhouse and partially

furnish it. Continue furnishing it with miniatures each Christmas. Grandpa can set up a railroad or race track. Miniatures may be added to these as well. Collectibles of dolls, bears, music boxes, trains, and cars can be expanded on gift giving occasions.

Gifts of stocks and bonds are nice for older children who understand the gift. Younger children like something tangible. If you are giving stocks and bonds to your grandchildren, include a small, inexpensive gift item for that hands-on appeal. Gift certificates or cash always bring a smile. Everyone likes to shop with their own money.

Handmade items are special gifts for special people. If you are good at making crafts, you may decide early in the year to make gifts for family members.

Books

Christmas is a time for books. *Rudolph* by Barbara Hazen (Golden) will be enjoyed in book, song, or video form. An inflatable plastic reindeer is easy to mail along with this much loved story. You can do the same with Clement Moore's classic, *The Night before Christmas.* Just add an inflatable Santa. The grandchildren will love hearing Grandpa's and Grandma's voices on tape, seeing the books, and receiving a holiday decoration too.

The Polar Express by Chris Van Allsburg (Houghton Mifflin) is a beautiful book about a boy's train ride to the North Pole, where Santa gives the boy a bell from a reindeer's harness. If your grandchild is old enough, a bell on a satin ribbon makes a nice accompaniment for this book and tape. A small wooden train set could also add hours of imaginative play.

Ernest Nister's Book of Christmas, illustrated by Jim Deesing (Philomel), has antique pictures that move. It is a gorgeous book that will delight the grandchild who has a special love for books. I recommend it for ages six and up. Small children might have trouble manipulating the tags and flaps. Of course, their eyes will light up when an adult reads the book to them. Grandchildren will love listening to the rhymes throughout.

Debby Boone's book, *Snow Angel,* illustrated by Gabriel Ferrer (Harvest House), is about a little girl and her grandfather. These kindred spirits, along with the Snow Angel, cause rainbow snow to fall. Together, they teach the townspeople to dream again. Be sure to mail some rainbow sprinkles, a can of icing, and some plain sugar cookies to decorate.

Another must read angel book is *Alabaster's Song* by Max Lucado, illustrated by Michael Garland (Word Kids). This is a Christmas story about a boy and the angel atop the Christmas tree. This wonderful story is also available on video. Max Lucado, along with his daughters, Jenna, Andrea, and Sara, has blessed us with another winning story, *The Crippled Lamb* (Word Kids). The beautiful illustrations are by Liz Bonham. This is truly a precious story that melts hearts.

Since long-distance grandparents and grandchildren are familiar with the postal service, include Janet and Allan Ahlberg's *The Jolly Christmas Postman* (Scholastic). This book is unique with its envelopes filled with surprises.

Add a little culture with Susan Titus Osborn's and Christine Tangvald's *Children around the World Celebrate Christmas* (Standard). The beautiful illustrations are by Jodie McCallum. You can expand on this theme by collecting Christmas ornaments from around the world for your grandchildren. Share recipes of Christmas cookies and pastries that originated in other countries. Make learning fun!

Take some time to browse through your bookstores (especially Christian bookstores), and visit your library. You will be enchanted with the beauty of the material that is available.

Crafts

Christmas wouldn't be Christmas if Grandma and the grandchildren didn't do a few craft projects. First on the agenda—gingerbread houses. Send the supplies, along with a videotape or written (illustrated) directions. Save pint milk cartons, or cut quart cartons down to the size of a whole graham cracker. Spread a paste of powdered sugar and water on the sides of the container. Apply a graham cracker to each of the four sides. Then add one square to each of the slanted sides to form a roof. Fill in across the top and on the sides with miniature marshmallows. Send gumdrops, licorice, candy canes, candy kisses, and other candies to decorate. Fun, fun, fun! These are just for looks, not to eat. Have the grandchildren spread some icing on the leftover crackers and decorate for a Christmas treat. Yum, yum, yum!

Creating cinnamon ornaments is another fun way to entertain grandchildren. These ornaments can be given as gifts, placed in baskets to scent your home, or used as Christmas tree ornaments.

Cinnamon Ornaments

4 ounces of ground cinnamon   2 tbsp white school glue
3/4 cup of applesauce

Mix the ingredients thoroughly. Roll out the dough, and cut out shapes with cookie cutters. Before the ornaments are completely dry, use a drinking straw to cut a hole in the top for hanging. Allow the ornaments to dry thoroughly. This may take several hours.

Do you want your house to be filled with the smells of an old-fashioned Christmas? Then make some homemade potpourri. Several days before you begin this project, buy some oranges, eat them, and save the peels. When the peels are dry, you are ready to begin. Spread an old sheet or tablecloth on your work table. Snip the orange peels into small pieces. Gather some fresh pine needles and cut them into small pieces. Add whole cloves and sprinkle with lots of ground cinnamon.

Cut squares of fabric the size of a potholder. Stitch two squares together on three sides and turn them inside out, forming a pocket. Cut a square of quilt batting to fit inside the pocket. Spoon your potpourri mixture onto one side of the batting. Slide the batting inside the pocket and slip stitch the open end. When hot dishes are placed on the square, it releases a wonderful, spicy aroma. Your grandchildren can make these potholders as gifts for teachers and other adults on their gift lists. Baskets may be lined with foil and filled with the potpourri. A holiday bow on the side adds a nice touch. These baskets may be given as gifts or placed throughout the house to give your Christmas that homemade scent. You may also heat a potpourri water mixture in a slow cooker.

The secret to making potpourri long distance is to send a video or written instructions along with the supplies. If your grandchildren have pine trees in their area, let them gather fresh needles. Ask Mom to shop for the oranges. Then all you have to do is package the spices, some precut fabric, needles and thread, and some precut batting. The project makes a memorable Christmas activity for the entire family.

Holiday Dishes

Do you have a favorite Christmas cookie or other treat that has become a tradition in your family? Then by all means write it on a recipe card and mail it to your grandchildren. The no-bake candies are great for the younger children.

Say the name of a certain food, and a bell rings "Christmas." The reverse is also true. Say "Christmas," and our thoughts turn to certain foods. When my children were small, we always had a special dinner on Christmas Eve for our immediate family. To stress that it was the Christ child's birthday, we celebrated with a birthday cake. Breakfast on Christmas morning always consisted of apple turnovers. The years have passed, and our adult children have their own homes. Still, we wouldn't think of having Christmas breakfast without apple turnovers. It's tradition! Other families have big sit-down meals, complete with Christmas dinnerware.

When your adult children establish their home and family, new traditions evolve. Some of your family traditions have had to change or will change over time. By now you know, change is inevitable. But it is nice to see some traditions carried over from one generation to the next.

The Christmas Story

Grandparents, encourage the establishment of spiritual traditions too. A tape of Grandpa reading the Christmas story is a treasure. The grandchildren can follow along in their Bibles as they hear the beloved family elder reading from God's Word. The tape can be done on a cassette or video. The cassette tape is nice because one can be made for each grandchild, and they can listen to it whenever they like.

Shepherd Bear, from my Touching Hearts gift line, helps a family share the Christmas story. The bear, dressed in a shepherd's costume, carries a shepherd's bag filled with memorabilia from the first Christmas night. Scripture references are given, and the entire extended family may participate in the reading of the selected passages. Bears may be ordered directly through Touching Hearts, P.O. Box 129, Westport, IN 47283.

You may also want to assign different verses from the Christmas story to each grandchild. Have each child write his or her passage on a page and then illustrate it. Assemble the pages into a family Christmas book. The pages may be photocopied so that each family member has a copy. Grandparents get to keep the original—a priceless treasure.

This Christmas, may the Christ child be born anew in the heart of every member of your extended family!

Journaling Pages

Our two-year-old grandson and I were looking at the nativity scene. "Who's that, Grandma?" he'd ask, as I pointed to each figure. When I pointed to Joseph, he quipped, "Josephs have to work!" meaning, dads go to work.

Wait 'til you hear what my grandchild said . . .

_____

_____

_____

_____

_____

_____

_____

Here's a bright idea for long-distance grandparenting . . .

_____

_____

_____

_____

_____

_____

_____

_____

Name of grandchild

Long-distance activity

Date completed

Name of grandchild

Long-distance activity

Date completed

Name of grandchild

Long-distance activity

Date completed

Name of grandchild

Long-distance activity

Date completed

Janet Colsher Teitsort is an author and elementary school teacher. She formerly taught first graders at South Decatur Elementary near Westport, Indiana, and now teaches language arts to sixth graders. Her other books include *Rainbows for Teachers, Treasures for Teachers, Seasons of Laughter for Teachers,* and *Quiet Times: Meditations for Today's Busy Woman.*